ISBN: 9798861983938

THE
ULTIMATE
CONFIDENCE
BOOK FOR GIRLS

5-MINUTE EXERCISES TO ELIMINATE SELF-DOUBT, POSITIVE
REINFORCEMENT, AND BECOMING FEARLESS OF FAILURE

MONICA J. PARK

Table of Contents

Introduction

Girls and boys have the same confidence when they're young. However, as girls grow into their adolescent phase, their confidence takes a considerable nosedive. When young, you are more open to taking risks and less scared of failures. However, as you get older, you're constantly warned about being careful, emphasizing perfection, and avoiding risks at all costs. Society further reinforces these beliefs and pushes girls to act a certain way, talk in a certain tone, and follow unwritten rules that only apply to girls.

Moreover, it doesn't help that girls develop physically and intellectually earlier than boys. This newfound emotional intelligence makes them more likely to avoid taking risks or exhibiting rash behavior. This way, girls excel in their lives, doing particularly well with academics and other aspects of life. Simultaneously, they start dealing with anxiety and self-doubt. This enhanced emotional intelligence makes them consciously aware of themselves. It doesn't help that parents and society expect them to be "good girls" and achieve unrealistic expectations.

The constant bombardment of picture-perfect lives on social media worsens matters. Young girls compare themselves with the unrealistic beauty standards set by models, actors, and influencers on social media, unaware that these are completely false representations. In contrast, boys become more confident with age because they're encouraged to try new things, take risks, and not be limited by their behavior. They risk and fail more easily, so their confidence improves. Yet, for girls of the same age, the same society unwittingly encourages them to be perfect and instill people-pleasing tendencies into them.

As a result, many girls form meek, quiet personalities with little to no confidence. They constantly doubt themselves, whether their appearance, the way they talk, their abilities, etc. This results in unhealthy coping mechanisms, often leaving them behind in life. Although girls can pursue their dreams today, they're often hindered by their inability to believe in themselves and establish themselves confidently and assertively. This book is the perfect guide for you if you struggle to maintain confidence every day. This book teaches you how to address the deep-rooted issues that give rise to the little voice of criticism and self-doubt within you. You'll discover practical techniques to manifest a confident personality and move through life with your head held high.

Chapter 1

Unmasking Self-Doubt

"Don't let others tell you what you can't do. Don't let the limitations of others limit your vision. If you can remove your self-doubt and believe in yourself, you can achieve what you never thought possible."

- Roy T. Bennett.

Confidence is one of the most powerful and attractive qualities a girl can have. It is believing in yourself and your abilities and skills to succeed in life. A confident person is aware of their strengths and weaknesses and is secure in who they are.

No matter how self-assured someone is, they can experience moments of self-doubt. When making a big decision, it is normal to question yourself and worry if things will go wrong. However, if you constantly have beliefs holding you back, your self-doubt consumes you and affects every area of your life.

There are various reasons behind your self-doubt, and you can only overcome it when you get to the source of your insecurities.

This chapter unmasks self-doubt so you can discover the reasons behind your limiting beliefs and conquer them once and for all.

WHAT IS SELF-DOUBT?

Self-doubt is low self-esteem and uncertainty about yourself, your decisions, your skills, and every other aspect of your life. This mindset stands in your way and holds you back from going after what you want, taking risks, and living the life you deserve.

Some people associate self-doubt with being humble. While it isn't desirable to boast about your achievements, you should still be proud of yourself and your abilities. William Shakespeare once said that self-doubt is a traitor. It is like having a two-faced friend who pretends they want the best for you but is secretly sabotaging your life.

People are neither born confident nor insecure. You develop either quality from school, family, or life experiences. If you have a healthy upbringing in a family that constantly supports and cheers for you, you learn to believe in yourself. On the other hand, childhood trauma, bullying, humiliation, criticism, or suffering from an attachment or anxiety disorder can lead to insecurity.

Experiencing negativity from an early age can influence your inner monologue and thoughts. You believe these negative comments to be true and let them dictate your life. Self-doubt can lead to many other issues like insecurity, lack of motivation, low self-worth, passiveness, low self-esteem, and people-pleasing.

RECOGNIZING LIMITING BELIEFS

Imagine you are at your friend's birthday, and everyone gets up to dance. They keep telling you to join them, but you say, "I don't have good moves, and I look weird when I dance." None of your friends can dance either. They are just having fun and aren't afraid to make a fool of themselves. What is the difference between you and them? They are confident and secure and don't care what other people think of them.

Limiting beliefs become second nature, so you might not know you have these thoughts. A few strategies can identify them so you can start your healing journey.

Self-Reflection

Reflect on your behavior and assess your attitude to get to the root of your limiting beliefs. Consider how you respond to different situations. For instance, how do you respond when someone says something hurtful or makes a mean comment about your clothes or weight? Confident people would speak up and calmly express they didn't appreciate these comments. However, if you walk away and keep your feelings to yourself, you let your limiting beliefs stop you.

You believe every time you stand up for yourself or express your feelings will result in conflict. However, it is good for your relationships to speak up whenever something bothers you. Even if you get into a conflict, it is normal. Friends, families, and couples fight, but this doesn't mean the end of your relationship. Your limiting beliefs are feeding you a false narrative, so don't listen to them.

Journaling

Write your personal and general beliefs in your journal, whether positive or negative. Think of your family, friends, school, job, relationships, and other beliefs about your life or the world around you.

Sit in a quiet room and avoid distractions so you can focus. Write down your feelings about each belief or the reasons behind them. Don't think too much, and write anything that comes to mind. When finished, read them carefully to recognize your limiting beliefs.

Write Down Your Challenges

Another approach is to write down all your daily challenges since they reflect your limiting beliefs and influence your life. Next to each challenge, write the belief associated with it. For instance, you can't find love because you believe people cheat, or all relationships end in heartbreak.

CAUSES OF YOUR LIMITING BELIEFS

Various reasons are behind your limiting beliefs, but they all stem from your fears and negative thinking. According to 2012 research conducted by psychologist Matthew Tyler Boden at the University of Illinois, limiting beliefs stem from rigid, inaccurate, and negative self-biased beliefs.

Limiting beliefs are damaging and unrealistic thoughts about yourself or the world, like "People are the worst. I don't trust anyone," "Everybody lies," or "If you want a successful career, you have to give up your social life."

These thoughts change how you view yourself and the world around you. They aim to keep you in your comfort zone and convince you they protect you from pain. For instance, if someone close to you betrays you, you will believe no one can be trusted to shield you from getting hurt again.

Limiting beliefs probably started in early childhood. They were simple thoughts you internalized, and over time and with new experiences, they became your core beliefs. Since these beliefs stem from your fears, they instill fear for the future or prevent you from seeing the good things in life. If you are about to embark on a new experience or make a decision, your negative thoughts will make you focus on everything that could go wrong instead of what can go right.

You can only understand and overcome these beliefs when you get to their roots.

Societal Expectations

Societal expectations substantially impact your beliefs, make you question your potential, and change your perceptions. Cultural or societal norms are unwritten rules made by society to determine what is acceptable and what isn't.

Who hasn't been in a situation where they wanted to say or do something but hesitated because it was against societal norms? These stereotypes guide your thoughts, choices, and decisions.

People want to feel they belong somewhere. Societal expectations make them feel safe and protected because they are on the side of the majority and live their lives based on what society deems right and accepted.

You should follow different societal expectations at home, school, or work and with your family, friends, neighbors, and strangers.

From early childhood, your family has taught you certain values that have influenced your core beliefs. They might not have instilled these beliefs in you on purpose. Perhaps they mentioned something once in front of you, or you watch how they respond to certain situations and unconsciously adopt these beliefs. For instance, if you hear your grandfather saying that rich people have it easy and they walk over everyone else, you will resent anyone who has money.

You are constantly taught various beliefs - simple ones like The Beatles are overrated, or life-altering ones like you are only as valuable as your education.

For instance, many societies believe college is necessary; otherwise, you are uneducated. You have adopted this belief, especially if your family members are college graduates. However, you want to become a singer and feel no reason to go to college. You struggle between what you want to do and what you feel obligated to do.

Past Experiences

Past experiences significantly impact your beliefs. If a bad incident has wounded you deeply, your limiting beliefs will be a defense mechanism or a shield protecting you from similar experiences in the future. For instance, when you were a child, you trusted your best friend with secrets no one else knew about your family. However, you had a fight one day, and she told everyone at school the secret. Since that day, you stopped confiding in anyone because you believed people would betray you sooner or later. You adopted this belief to protect yourself from future pain.

Every experience is associated with a feeling that can stay in your memory for years. It is a constant reminder of the negative experience. For instance, you were learning to drive and almost had an accident and were extremely terrified. Whenever someone suggests teaching you to drive, you refuse because you remember this terrifying feeling.

Internalized Negativity

As the name suggests, internalized negativity is negative thoughts about yourself but focused internally. It is a coping mechanism where you hold in your anger, stress, and upsetting situations because you want to handle them privately. You fear that releasing these feelings will burden others or they will judge you. Internalized negativity can lead to anger, grief, isolation, insecurity, loneliness, self-loathing, and self-doubt.

Since you keep your problems to yourself, not sharing them with your family or friends, your issues will appear more serious and intense than they really are. For instance, your boyfriend is acting differently. Rather than asking him if anything is wrong, you internalize your feelings; they intensify and affect your beliefs. You believe he is cheating on you or going to break up with you. However, if you talked to him, you would have discovered he had a fight with his parents and was ashamed to tell you about it.

When you talk about your problems with a loved one, they can point out something you haven't noticed or explain the situation isn't as serious as you think. In other words, internalizing makes you focus on the negative and worst-case scenarios, but a friend will look at it from a different perspective and show you the positive side you missed.

Education

Your friends, family, classmates, or teachers can impact your thoughts. If your parents have certain beliefs, you can adopt and believe them to be true. For instance, if your mother tells you that you will never be happy until you get married and have children, you will live an unfulfilled life until you meet "the one." Even if you succeed in your career and achieve your dreams, you will never be happy because of the belief your mother instilled in you. While this belief isn't true and can damage your self-esteem, you have learned it since childhood, so it is a fact.

Another example: You love singing and have dreams of becoming a singer. However, your music teacher said you have a bad voice. Since that day, you haven't been able to sing, not even in the bathroom. You let one person's opinion change your life and prevent you from doing something you love. Most people are inclined to adopt a certain belief if someone they respect and look up to teaches it to them.

INTROSPECTIVE EXERCISES AND THOUGHT-PROVOKING QUESTIONS

Try these exercises and questions for better insight into your self-doubt.

Questions

Whenever you experience self-doubt or limiting belief, ask yourself these questions and write down the answers.

- How do you feel right now?
- How long have you been feeling this way?
- Does your self-doubt stem from perception or facts? (Write down these perceptions or facts)
- Read them out loud. How do they make you feel?
- Do you need to work on yourself to become a more secure person?
- What do you need to do to make real changes in your life?
- What is preventing you from making these changes?
- What should you do to get rid of these obstacles?
- What do you believe will happen if you don't change the beliefs behind your self-doubt?
- How will your life change when you get rid of your negative thoughts?

After answering these questions, reflect on what you wrote for a few minutes.

Exercise

Whenever you experience self-doubt, say out loud, "Stop." Pause for a moment, then ask yourself why you have these thoughts and whether your fears are reasonable. Think about your answers and identify where these thoughts stem from.

HOW TO OVERCOME LIMITING BELIEFS

You can overcome these limiting beliefs. You merely need to believe in yourself and be ready to fight the negativity. These strategies are powerful and effective, but you must be patient and don't give up until you fully get rid of your self-doubt.

Question Your Limiting Beliefs

Limiting beliefs can seem meaningless and have less influence over you when you question them. In other words, ask yourself whether they are based on something real or logical. For instance, you believe if you tell your best friend you are upset with her, she will never talk to you again. Ask yourself, "Does my belief sound logical?" It doesn't make sense that someone who loves you and has been with you for years will cut you out of their life because you told them they hurt your feelings

Make it a habit to question every belief you have and create different what-if scenarios and imagine their outcomes. What if I told my best friend how I was feeling, and she apologized for hurting me? What if she didn't upset me on purpose? What if it's all a misunderstanding? By questioning your beliefs, you will realize there are more positive and logical outcomes than negative ones in your head.

Is Your Belief Helping You?

There is a reason you hold on to your limiting beliefs. At one time in your life, they helped and impacted your life in a good way. Maybe a belief has prevented you from failure or protected you from pain. Some people like to be victims of their limiting beliefs or adopt them because they attract attention or make them feel special. For instance, a pretty girl who uses her looks to get special treatment keeps saying, "It isn't fair people only judge me for my looks." She clearly holds on to these beliefs to attract attention to her looks.

Whenever you have a limiting belief that has served you well in the past, ask yourself if it still helps you and is worth holding on to it.

Challenge Negative Self-Talk

Since your limiting beliefs stem from negative self-talk, you can challenge and reframe them using positive thoughts and affirmations. Negative thoughts aren't real since they are based on your fears and insecurities. When you challenge them, they won't have power over you. Whenever you believe you can't do something, think of when you succeeded in achieving your goals. For instance, you believe you won't lose weight. Challenge these thoughts with different methods. Ask yourself questions like: Why can't I lose weight? All people who work out and eat healthy have lost weight, so why can't I?

Also, change your negative self-talk. Rather than saying, "I can't lose weight," say, "I can lose weight," or "I have what it takes to lose weight." Always talk about yourself using positive statements like, I am smart, I am confident, or I am funny. Even if you don't believe these thoughts, keep repeating them; in time, they will replace negative beliefs.

Affirmations are powerful and will change your thought pattern. They are positive statements you repeat daily to challenge a negative mentality.

Here are a few examples:

- My negative thoughts have no control over me
- I am not my insecurities or fears
- I don't have to be perfect. I am great the way I am
- My mistakes don't define me

- I let go of my limiting beliefs and self-doubt and embraced confidence
- I choose gratitude over fear
- I choose to challenge my limiting beliefs
- I choose to silence my inner critic with self-love
- No one can influence my beliefs but me
- I deserve love today and every day
- I am in control of my thoughts and my life
- My head is filled with positive thoughts
- I am at peace
- My happiness is my choice
- I overcome all the challenges in my life
- I will not think of anything that hurts me
- I choose myself
- I trust that I will always make the right decisions
- I am surrounded by love and light
- I have a positive attitude toward my life
- I choose hope over self-doubt
- I give myself permission to be myself
- I handle everything with confidence
- Disappointments won't bring me down

You Choose Your Beliefs

Now that you know how to challenge your thoughts and replace them with positive ones, apply them to your life. For instance, you believe that if you learn to drive, you will get into an accident. After you adopt new beliefs, take a driving lesson to prove to yourself that nothing bad will happen.

Overcoming your limited beliefs isn't only about changing your thoughts. You must live your life and put your new positive attitude into action.

No one forces you to adopt these limited beliefs. It's your choice. They are a comfort zone you are afraid to leave because you don't know what's on the other side. Understand that your self-doubt is only in your head. It doesn't have any power over you; you are in control. Once you discover where your negative thoughts come from, you will unmask your self-doubt, come face to face with it, and get rid of the enemy holding you back.

KEY TAKEAWAYS

- Self-doubt stems from your negative thoughts
- Your limiting beliefs will hold you back if you let them
- Society, past experiences, and the people in your life can shape your core beliefs
- You can overcome limiting beliefs if you dig deep and discover their causes

Chapter 2

Embracing Your Inner Strength

"The power you have is to be the best version of yourself you can be so that you can create a better world."

- Ashley Rickards

In this day and age, the world is moving at such a fast pace it's hard to keep track of the changes taking place. However, you have the power to navigate it with confidence and self-assurance. You merely need to see yourself in a positive light and embrace your capabilities and imperfections. You don't have to be perfect because your uniqueness makes you special. When you feel confident, handling academic pressure, resisting peer coercion, and making responsible choices about alcohol, drugs, and relationships becomes easier. Your "can do" attitude will be your superpower, empowering you to stand up for yourself in adulthood and skillfully manage various aspects of life.

So, how can you become a motivated, enthusiastic, and optimistic "can-do" girl? It starts with knowing you are truly important and loved. Surround yourself with supportive people who provide positive feedback and help you expand your horizons. Embrace the love and care you receive because it fuels your self-esteem and motivation. But remember, it's essential for others to avoid excessive blame, nagging, or fault-finding. You don't need constant criticism; it only harms your mental health and confidence. Instead, focus on constructive feedback to encourage growth. Nobody's perfect, and mistakes are part of learning and growing.

If you ever face hurtful words or actions, know it's not your fault. Shielding yourself from negativity is a way to protect your self-respect. Don't let harmful words bring you down or make you question your worth. Surround yourself with positive influences, and let go of anyone who undermines your confidence. Seek love and support from those who genuinely care about you and show it through actions and words. Embrace the love that resonates with you; don't settle for anything less. This chapter is about looking within to find what makes you proud of yourself. You'll be surprised at how different your attitude will be once you recognize yourself for the beautiful, confident young woman you are.

STOP COMPARING YOURSELF

First and foremost, it's time to break free from the trap of comparison. Comparing yourself to others steals away your joy and hinders your path to genuine self-confidence. You deserve to embrace your uniqueness without constantly measuring up to those around you. So, let's take a step toward building that confidence. Start by identifying your comparison triggers. These triggers could be the people you follow on social media, the high-end retail store near your house, or a friend who loves to brag about their achievements. Take a moment to jot down these triggers, acknowledging what makes you feel inadequate or insecure. Now, it's time to take charge and reduce these triggers. For instance, if social media is a culprit, dedicate time to unfollow anyone who undermines your self-worth. Surround yourself with positive and inspiring content that uplifts you instead. As for a certain clothing store, consider limiting your visits or finding other ways to avoid temptation.

FOCUS ON YOUR STRENGTHS

People remember the bad more than the good; this preoccupation with their failures can detrimentally impact their confidence. However, focusing on your strengths is a powerful remedy to boost your self-esteem. An effective confidence-building exercise is reflecting on what you have accomplished in life, reaching as far back as you can remember, and even recalling small victories like that spelling bee you won in 5th grade. Writing down your achievements creates a valuable reference to remind you of your greatness whenever you need a pick-me-up.

Another way to build confidence is by acknowledging and celebrating your talents and skills. Whether it's as simple as making homemade coffee that rivals any coffee shop or as complex as running a successful business generating substantial revenue, these strengths are what make you exceptional. Embracing and honoring them is key to recognizing your worth and value.

If you're unsure about your strengths or want to explore yourself further, consider these journal prompts for self-discovery:

- What are three accomplishments I'm most proud of, and why?
- Describe a challenging situation I faced and how I successfully navigated it
- What activities make me lose track of time and bring me joy?
- List five qualities my friends and family admire in me
- What do I consider my unique talents? How can I use them to make a positive impact?
- Recall a moment when I overcame self-doubt and achieved something remarkable
- How do I handle setbacks? What can I learn from these experiences?
- Describe when I helped someone else succeed or feel better about themselves
- What new skills or knowledge do I want to acquire? Why are they important to me?

DITCH PERFECTIONISM

How many times have you held yourself back because you felt you weren't ready or good enough? Maybe you refrained from running a marathon, convinced you needed to be in better shape first. Perhaps you missed out on a promotion because you doubted your qualifications. It's not uncommon to agonize over tasks for hours, endlessly editing and perfecting, but this perfectionist approach often takes a toll on your confidence and hinders progress.

It's time to break free from the clutches of perfectionism and put an end to overanalyzing everything. Instead of hesitating, go ahead and sign up for that marathon you've been eyeing. Pursue that promotion confidently and show your boss what you're capable of. Submit that report knowing you've done your best, and trust your abilities. Remember, perfection is an elusive goal, and waiting for everything to be flawless before taking action can lead to missed opportunities and unrealized potential. Embrace imperfection, take a leap of faith, and surprise yourself with what you can achieve when you let go of the constraints of perfectionism.

REWIRE YOUR NEGATIVE THOUGHTS

Every day, people have an average of over 6,000 thoughts swirling in their minds. Sometimes, it's that inner critic's voice that is the loudest. But fear not; morning affirmations are a powerful tool to counteract this negative chatter. Engaging in morning affirmations is one of the most effective confidence-building exercises you can adopt. By speaking positive, empowering statements to yourself, you can silence the little critic within and set the tone for a more positive and focused day ahead. For instance, if you believe you're scatterbrained, your morning affirmation might be, "My mind is clear and focused. Nothing can deter me from achieving my goals." The beauty of affirmations lies in their ability to reshape negative beliefs you might have about yourself, fostering a more encouraging and optimistic mindset.

SMILE AND MAKE EYE CONTACT

Even in moments when you might not feel like it, simply smiling and making eye contact with others can significantly boost your confidence. This simple act sends a powerful signal to those around you, indicating that you are approachable and open to communication, creating a positive and friendly atmosphere. Not only does it put others at ease, but it also profoundly impacts your self-assurance. With practice, this behavior becomes increasingly natural and effortless. As smiling and maintaining eye contact becomes a habit, you'll notice how it becomes second nature, further enhancing your ability to connect with people and exude confidence in various social situations.

SET A GOAL

A remarkable sense of empowerment comes with setting and successfully accomplishing a goal. However, with a multitude of goals swirling in your mind, it can be challenging to take action on a specific one. So, here's a fun and effective approach: turn one of your goals into a challenge. Whether a small goal, like learning a new financial term you're unfamiliar with, or a more substantial aspiration, like maxing out your retirement account for the year, the key is to make it an exciting challenge. By framing it this way, you infuse enthusiasm and motivation into the pursuit, turning the journey toward your goal into an enjoyable adventure. Remember, the beauty of this approach is that the possibilities are endless. Dream big and aim high; let your imagination soar without limits.

PRIORITIZE SELF-DISCIPLINE

Self-discipline is mastering control over your emotions and behaviors. It is a powerful force propelling you to stay committed to your goals, even when they seem ambitious and challenging, such as achieving financial freedom or purchasing your dream house. You can implement several effective strategies to enhance your self-discipline. Firstly, consider setting small, manageable goals aligning with your larger objectives. This incremental approach allows you to build momentum and confidence as you achieve each milestone, ultimately leading to realizing your bigger aspirations.

Another valuable method to strengthen self-discipline is to immerse yourself in self-improvement literature. These resources offer invaluable insight and techniques to overcome obstacles and maintain focus on your journey toward success. Moreover, having an accountability partner can be a game-changer. When you have someone to share your goals with and who holds you accountable, you become more driven and committed to staying on track. Their support and encouragement can significantly boost your self-discipline and keep you motivated throughout the process.

TAKE YOURSELF ON A DATE

The path to loving others deeply and authentically starts with loving yourself. A beautiful way to cultivate this self-love is by going on a date with yourself. Dedicate 30 minutes or an hour each week to genuinely get to know and appreciate the amazing person you are. During this time, explore your likes and dislikes without judgment. Embrace your thoughts and feelings, getting comfortable with your own company. Engage in activities that pique your interest or try something new you've always wanted to experience. This journey of self-discovery and self-appreciation can be one of the most enriching confidence-building activities you'll ever embark upon.

PRACTICE SHARING YOUR OPINIONS

For those who identify as introverted and find it challenging to speak out, making an effort to develop and express your opinions more openly is crucial. Even if you doubt your ability to share your thoughts eloquently and succinctly, practice makes all the difference. Start by saying your opinions out loud to a trusted partner or yourself in front of a mirror. The more you verbalize your thoughts, the more confidence you'll gradually build in expressing them to others. This practice is a stepping stone toward overcoming the hesitations holding you back from speaking up. Sharing your opinions is a vital activity in building self-esteem. It allows you to assert your identity, communicate your ideas, and contribute to discussions confidently.

START THINKING LIKE A CONFIDENT WOMAN

Imagine the most confident woman you know, someone who exudes self-assurance in every aspect of her life. Now, whenever you find yourself faced with a daunting or intimidating situation, take a moment to ask yourself, "What would she do in this situation?" Channeling her mindset, act on the instinctive response that comes to mind. This technique might resemble "faking it 'til you make it," but it stands as one of the most effective confidence-building exercises to practice.

Emulating her approach shifts your focus from negative thoughts and self-doubt, empowering you to take bold and courageous action. When you envision yourself in the shoes of that confident woman, you draw strength from her example and embody the same assertiveness. As you consistently practice this exercise, you'll notice a transformation within yourself, growing more at ease with facing challenges and embracing opportunities for growth.

PRACTICE SELF-CARE

While looks certainly aren't everything, feeling confident in your skin is essential for overall well-being. If you feel less than enthusiastic about your appearance, it might be time to invest in self-care. Allocate money in your budget to refresh your wardrobe, treating yourself to new clothing that makes you feel great. Consider getting a manicure or pampering yourself with a facial you've been eager to try. Engaging in these self-care activities boosts your confidence and enhances your relaxation and well-being. The power of self-care should not be underestimated; it stands as one of the most effective confidence-building exercises available. When you prioritize taking care of yourself and feeling good about your appearance, you radiate positive energy reflecting on how you carry yourself and interact with others.

SHOW YOUR BODY SOME LOVE

The benefits of regular exercise on self-confidence are well-established. Engaging in physical activity boosts self-assurance and is a powerful stress reliever since it releases endorphins and helps you momentarily escape life's daily worries. The key lies in finding an activity you truly enjoy, something sparking joy and excitement within you. Whether dancing in your kitchen, hiking through nature's wonders, or starting a garden in your backyard, the key is to move your body that feels fun and fulfilling. Dedicating around 30 minutes a day to your preferred exercise can work wonders for your overall well-being. Pair this with a healthy, balanced diet, and you have a winning combination enhancing your physical health and significantly contributing to building self-esteem.

BE KIND TO YOURSELF

Getting to know yourself is a powerful journey leading to greater self-acceptance and confidence. Take time to explore what truly makes you happy and what you value most in life. Writing these reflections in a journal can be a helpful way to gain clarity and deepen your understanding of yourself.

- Challenge unkind thoughts you have about yourself. When negative self-talk arises, ask yourself if you would treat a friend the same way. Practicing self-compassion and speaking to yourself with kindness is essential for building self-esteem.

- Speak positive affirmations to yourself, even if it feels strange initially. Some people find it beneficial to say these affirmations in front of a mirror. Over time, this practice fosters a more positive self-image and boosts self-confidence.
- Learn to say no, when necessary, assertively. Remember, it's okay to prioritize your well-being and not always please others at the expense of your happiness.
- Avoid the trap of comparing yourself to others, especially on social media or online communities. Remember, people choose what they present online, which might not reflect their whole truth. Focus on your journey and growth.
- Engage in self-kindness and self-care. Doing something nice for yourself, whether cooking your favorite meal or indulging in a hobby, can uplift your spirits and reinforce self-love.
- Recognize that nobody's life is perfect, and everyone has their insecurities. Embrace the idea that we all have our struggles and imperfections, and it's what makes us human.

TRY TO RECOGNIZE POSITIVES

Celebrating your successes, no matter how small, is a wonderful way to nurture self-esteem. Take the time to praise yourself for every achievement, whether going for a refreshing walk or tidying up your space. Acknowledging these accomplishments reinforces a positive self-image and encourages further growth. Learn to accept compliments graciously, and consider saving them from revisiting during moments of self-doubt or low self-esteem. Reminding yourself of the kind words others have shared can be a powerful source of affirmation and confidence.

Seek feedback from others by asking what they appreciate or like about you. Sometimes, people can recognize qualities and strengths you might overlook or underestimate. Writing a list of things you like about yourself is a profound exercise in self-love. Include skills you've acquired, kind acts you've done for others, and positive traits you possess. This list becomes a valuable reminder of your worth and uniqueness.

Maintaining a gratitude diary is a powerful practice directly countering overwhelm and catastrophic thinking. Focusing on what you're grateful for shifts your perspective to a more positive and balanced outlook, significantly impacting your overall well-being.

BUILD A SUPPORT NETWORK

Opening up and talking to someone you trust can be incredibly beneficial. Having a supportive person listen to you and show genuine care gives comfort and relief. If confiding in someone close feels challenging, consider reaching out to a helpline where you can speak to someone anonymously and receive understanding and empathy. Focusing on positive relationships is essential for nurturing self-esteem. It is not always possible to control every social interaction but prioritize spending time with people who uplift and appreciate you for who you are. Surrounding yourself with positive influences profoundly impacts your self-perception and overall well-being. Exploring peer support can also be incredibly helpful. Connecting with individuals who share similar experiences or challenges can foster a sense of belonging and provide a supportive network. Online communities can be a valuable source of understanding and encouragement.

In the journey of life, you will often encounter moments of self-discovery and empowerment. As you navigate the ups and downs, remember finding yourself is an ongoing process filled with growth and learning. Embrace the uniqueness of who you are, and never underestimate the power you hold within. Believe in yourself, for you possess a strength and resilience that knows no bounds. Trust in your abilities, your dreams, and your worth. Surround yourself with positive influences, and let your inner voice be of self-compassion and encouragement. You can achieve greatness, break barriers, and make a difference in the world. Embrace your individuality, celebrate your accomplishments, and uplift others along the way.

KEY TAKEAWAYS

- Embrace your uniqueness and recognize you don't need to be perfect
- Stop comparing yourself to others; reduce triggers that make you feel inadequate
- Focus on your strengths and achievements to build confidence
- Ditch perfectionism and embrace imperfection, taking action instead of waiting for flawless outcomes
- Use morning affirmations to counteract negative self-talk
- Smile and make eye contact to boost confidence and create positive interactions
- Set goals and turn them into exciting challenges to enhance motivation
- Prioritize self-discipline through small, manageable goals and self-improvement resources
- Take yourself on a date to cultivate self-love and appreciation
- Practice sharing your opinions to develop confidence in expressing yourself
- Think like a confident woman in challenging situations to shift focus away from self-doubt
- Practice self-care, including exercise and a healthy diet, to boost overall well-being and confidence
- Be kind to yourself, challenge negative thoughts, and avoid comparison
- Recognize and celebrate your successes, accept compliments, and maintain a gratitude diary
- Build a supportive network with positive influences and consider peer support
- Embrace the journey of self-discovery, believe in your abilities, dreams, and worth, and uplift others along the way

Chapter 3

Embracing Your Unique Beauty

"Beauty begins the moment you decide to be yourself."
- Coco Chanel

What is beauty? The meaning of beauty has changed throughout the years. Look at pictures of women from past decades, and you will notice that women's bodies, hair, makeup, and teeth have undergone many transformations. For instance, in the nineties, women had thin eyebrows, but nowadays, they prefer thick and full eyebrows. Beauty trends change rapidly, so what was considered sexy ten years ago might be unattractive now.

Girls feel pressured to keep up with these trends, especially since social media platforms like Instagram have set unrealistic standards for beauty. Whenever you look at a celebrity picture, the word perfect often comes to mind. They have pearly white teeth, full eyebrows, thick hair, flawless skin, and toned bodies. Naturally, you can't help comparing yourself to them. Even though many of these pictures are filtered or heavily edited, they impact girls' self-image and alter their perception of beauty.

No matter how many trends surface or how the definition of attractiveness changes, one thing remains the same; there is still something lovely and innocent about natural beauty. People will see something captivating in you and embrace your unique beauty if you ignore social media and the insane beauty standards.

PRESSURES AND INFLUENCES ON YOUR SELF-PERCEPTIONS

Girls are constantly under pressure to look pretty. Social media, TV shows, and your peers influence your perception of beauty and body image. From a young age, girls are judged on their looks. Many feel they have to look or dress a certain way to be deemed beautiful. Since beauty standards have become unrealistic, many girls have low self-esteem, stress, anxiety, and depression.

Societal Pressures

Society has convinced girls that their value is associated with their looks. It has put unrealistic expectations on them that can be summed up in one word, perfection. All over the world, beauty standards have become ridiculous.

Girls are expected to be perfect all the time. They must wear makeup, wear stylish and fitting clothes, and their hair should always be properly styled. If you don't give your appearance the proper attention, you will often hear comments like, "Are you okay? You look tired today," or "You don't look like yourself today." You are expected to leave the house looking like you have spent hours getting ready. Even the "natural" or no makeup look many celebrities adopt takes time to achieve and involves many beauty products.

Society doesn't want girls to be themselves and has determined what their ideal features should look like. Every girl should have pouty lips, big eyes, a sharp nose, a perfect jawline, and a fit body. Hence, many girls resort to plastic surgery to achieve this unrealistic look.

Many have become unsatisfied with their appearance, especially when constantly judged by their family or peers. For instance, a mother obsessed with being skinny results in her kids growing up with an unhealthy body image. She will push them to watch what they eat and teach them their self-worth is associated with their looks. They will believe that "fat" is a bad word. Although having a healthy weight is encouraged to protect from various diseases, you shouldn't feel pressured to be skinny to fit insane beauty standards. Your goal is to be healthy and happy with your body.

Gone are the days when people believed beauty was in the eyes of the beholder. Beauty used to be subjective. Every person had an idea of what was attractive and what wasn't. However, nowadays, there are guidelines for a girl's appearances, which must be followed to be part of their communities.

The truth many people don't say out loud is that society is wrong. Changing yourself to follow society's rules is extremely irrational and backward. Many of these standards come from the beauty industry wanting you to be unsatisfied with your look to buy their products.

It is normal for girls to practice self-care and look pretty as it gives them confidence, but caving into societal pressures isn't healthy.

Media Influences

Girls have always paid attention to their looks. In past centuries, women looked beautiful and flawless yet maintained a natural appearance since plastic surgery and Botox weren't common as today. However, they weren't obsessed with their looks or beauty trends.

The main reasons behind girls' current obsession with their looks are the media and social media. According to a study conducted by the Prince's Trust and the Education Policy Institute, 29% of young girls were unsatisfied with their looks and body. The research also found that 40% of girls who spend long periods on social media were prone to depression.

Have you recently seen a movie, TV show, or advertisement that didn't feature attractive people? Even storylines in everything you see on TV focus on beauty. For instance, a guy ignores a girl throughout the movie until she gets a makeover and wears a nice dress. All of a sudden, he realizes how amazing she is. Unattractive people are usually the main character's friends or play non-significant roles in the story.

Hollywood celebrities are the first to adopt beauty trends. Female celebrities are hailed for their beauty and toned bodies. When they get plastic surgery or lose weight, they are often celebrated by the media for their "amazing transformation."

Fashion brands like Victoria's Secret only work with skinny and gorgeous models. When you next go to a mall, pay attention to the adverts. You will only see pictures of beautiful people. The media largely impacts people and their perceptions. However, nothing has a more powerful impact than social media.

Celebrities and influencers constantly post images of themselves with perfect hair, body, makeup, etc. Some share pictures when in bed and claim to have just woken up when clearly, they're wearing makeup or using filters. What's worse is many use the hashtag "no filter" to prove this is their natural look. Firstly, no one wakes up looking like that, so the natural or no-filter look is a lie. Besides, most celebrities have work done; those who didn't have plastic surgery had Botox or filler injections, hair treatments, eyebrows microblading, and got veneers. So, these images are fake since they've altered their look one way or another. Many celebrities, like the Kardashians, edit their photos before posting them on social media to hide their flaws or to appear skinnier or prettier than they are.

This obsession with filtered images is responsible for "Snapchat dysphoria," a body image disorder making people obsessed with looking like their filtered images. Many plastic surgeons have stated they get requests from patients to make them look like filtered Snapchat images.

Social media is a big lie that has put unnecessary pressure on you for their gain. Nowadays, girls don't go out to have fun anymore. They get dressed up and pick a nice place solely for taking pictures to post online and show people how great they look.

Moreover, social media is filled with cyber bullies. They hide behind their screens and leave hurtful comments mocking people's appearance. A few celebrities have quit social media because cyber-bullying and negativity damage their mental health. When young girls read comments like, "You are fat" or "You are ugly," it destroys their self-esteem and causes severe depression.

The more you expose yourself to social media, the more obsessed you will be with your looks. You will believe you'll never measure up and see flaws in yourself that aren't there, causing you to develop compulsive behavior or eating disorders.

Social media is a toxic place, slowly destroying your mental health, even if you aren't aware of it. The images you see on social media are traps. Nothing is what it seems. It is a fictional world people online create to show an unreal image of their looks and lives. Use social media to only connect with your loved ones, and don't allow it to ruin your self-esteem.

Comparison Traps

Social media and society's unrealistic beauty standards have led girls to fall into comparison traps. They often believe they aren't pretty or skinny enough compared to the pictures on Instagram. Don't feel bad comparing yourself to other girls; everyone does it sometimes. Nowadays, when you constantly sit behind your screen watching other people's pictures, you can't help but make comparisons.

An interesting theory called "Social Comparison" suggests that people often compare themselves to others to assess their lives. Social comparison has two types: downward comparison and upward comparison. Downward comparison is when you compare yourself to the less fortunate and feel grateful for your life and all your blessings. Upward comparison is comparing yourself to people you believe are more beautiful or live better lives than you. This comparison leads to unrealistic expectations, low self-esteem, and insecurity.

Comparisons can be helpful if they show how lucky you are or push you to make positive life changes. However, if they make you feel bad about yourself and question your looks and body image, you have fallen into comparison traps harming your self-esteem.

If you pay attention to how you talk about yourself, you will notice you don't only compare yourself to celebrities but to your friends and also others. For instance, you notice one of your best friends is skinny even though she eats junk food and sweets almost every day and doesn't work out. Yet you can't lose weight even though you watch what you eat. Or when you go out with your friends, you can't help but notice if they look better than you. Even if you are prettier and have a nicer body, you still feel less because you don't know your self-worth.

The only person you should compare yourself to is you. When you accept and love yourself for who you are, you will not be affected by other girls you deem prettier or skinnier.

THOUGHT-PROVOKING QUESTIONS

No matter how many people tell you that you are beautiful, have a nice smile, or have lovely hair, you won't believe them if you are preoccupied with the images online. You are the only person who can change your mind and make you believe society's beauty standards are ridiculous. You must distance yourself from social media for a few minutes and ask yourself these questions. You could also discuss them with your friends, siblings, or family.

- What is body image?
- Why do I need to have a positive body image?
- Where does my negative body image come from?
- How can I learn to accept myself?
- How does social media and media influence my body image?
- How can I reduce the impact of social media on my self-image?
- How can I embrace my unique beauty?
- How do I feel about my body?
- Do I like the way I look?
- Does my body reflect my true personality?
- Do I allow societal norms to influence my self-image?
- Do I feel pressured to lose weight?
- Do I compare myself to others? How does it make me feel?
- Do I believe societal beauty standards are realistic?
- Does how I look affect my self-esteem?

EMPOWERING AND SELF-ACCEPTANCE ACTIVITIES

You can do certain daily activities to feel empowered and accept your looks and body.

Use Positive Affirmations

- I am perfect the way I am
- There is more to life than looks
- I accept my body
- I am aware of my self-worth
- I am beautiful
- I respect and love my body
- I appreciate my body and care for it
- My body is my home; it gives me life, and I am grateful for it
- My body is fabulous
- My body gives me strength and power

Compliment Yourself

When you wake up every day, point at a random part of your face or body and compliment yourself. Before you leave the house, look in the mirror and say something nice about your looks or outfit, like, "This is a stylish outfit," or "I look gorgeous today."

Make Promises to Yourself

Treat your body like a friend you want to protect from negativity. Write down a list of promises to make to your body and keep them.

- I promise I will never disrespect or speak negatively about my body
- I will drink enough water, eat healthy, and work out to keep my body strong
- I will give my body the sleep it needs every day
- I will never compare my body to others

Use Social Media Differently

When scrolling on Instagram, don't only pay attention to the pictures. Focus on the captions and look for the meaning behind them.

Let It Go

Write down on a piece of paper the unrealistic beauty and body-image standards you expect from yourself, then burn the piece of paper, tear it up, or throw it away to let them go.

THE SIGNIFICANCE OF SELF-CARE

Self-care is practicing healthy habits like reading or getting enough sleep to improve your physical, emotional, and mental health. It is taking a break from your responsibilities and social media and adopting activities to better your life. It allows you to focus on yourself and the present moment so you don't concern yourself with others.

Self-care is different for each person. For some, it is going out with friends and having fun. For others, it's a relaxing massage or reading a good book. Find activities that make you happy and relaxed and incorporate them into your daily routine.

When you care for your body, it will take care of you. Practice healthy habits like drinking enough water and exercising. You will feel more refreshed and active.

Self-care allows you to slow down and focus inward. By distancing yourself from social media and the external noises telling you how to look, you will see these beauty standards from a different perspective. Self-care makes you happy and relaxed, love yourself and gives you peace of mind.

Lack of self-care can lead to many issues like stress, frustration, low self-esteem, and depression.

STRATEGIES TO FOSTER BODY POSITIVITY

Understand Beauty Is Skin-Deep

You are more than just your looks or body image. Stop obsessing over your appearance and focus on other aspects of yourself. Think of everything that makes you special, like your kindness, passion, or sense of humor.

Give Your Body a Gift

Love your body by caring for it. Give it gifts like self-care to promote positive body image and relaxation, like napping, going on a hike, taking a bubble bath, or spending time outdoors.

Embrace Positive Body Images

Check websites or apps with positive messages rather than spending all your time on Instagram or other social media platforms. You can read articles or quotes about positive body image, listen to songs about self-acceptance, or read a self-help book.

Accept Your Uniqueness

Nowadays, many celebrities and influencers look the same. Girls don't wear clothes or makeup to express their personal style; they merely copy others. How can you stand out or feel special when all girls look alike? Don't compare yourself to others; there is a reason you are different, and you should be proud and embrace it. In a world where many girls choose to look fake, be proud of your natural beauty.

When former supermodel Gisele Bündchen started her career, she was a teenager. People would often point out her physical flaws, like her big nose. However, Bündchen didn't let these comments get to her and embraced her unique features. She said that her big nose comes with a big personality. Now she is one of the most beautiful and successful models in the world.

Do you think she would have become successful if she had given in to peer pressure and had a nose job? Her unique beauty made her interesting and encouraged the biggest fashion houses in the world to work with her.

It might sound like a cliché, but each person is beautiful in their way. So, the next time you look at a friend's or celebrity's photo, be grateful for your face and body because they are yours and set you apart from everyone else.

Be around Positive People

Spend time with friends or family who lift you up and remind you how beautiful and amazing you are. Steer clear from people who judge or mock you.

Focus on Being Healthy

Give your body what it needs by exercising, eating healthy, and staying hydrated. However, your goal should be your health, not being skinny. You give your body fuel to nourish it so it has the strength to take you places and to work hard to achieve your goals. Be grateful for what your body does for you instead of its appearance or weight.

You are beautiful. Social media and society's beauty standards are wrong; hence they keep changing every few years. One day skinny eyebrows are pretty, and the next, they are ugly. You can't keep changing yourself based on what society dictates. Be your own person and embrace your unique beauty. Ignore the outside noises and learn to love yourself and your flaws. Understand that no one is perfect and see beyond the lies social media feeds you.

Don't give social media power over you; understand that the images online are fake. If you want to see real and unedited beauty, look in the mirror.

KEY TAKEAWAYS

- Society and social media influence how you see yourself
- Most images you see on social media platforms are fake or altered
- Society's definition of beauty is unhealthy and wrong
- If you accept yourself, you won't be vulnerable to societal influences
- Practice self-care and learn to love your body

Chapter 4

Cultivate Self-Compassion

"To be nobody - but yourself - in a world which is doing its best, night and day, to make you everybody else - means to fight the hardest battle which any human being can fight."

– E.E. Cummings

Treating others with compassion is a virtue and a trait you hope to cultivate within yourself, your children, and your broader community. However, you forget that the same compassion you are so generous to impart upon others should be shared with you, too. You forget that humility or self-awareness does not necessarily mean beating yourself up over every minor infraction. It's a pretty easy way to destroy your self-confidence and prevents you from building a solid ground for self-esteem.

Developing a positive self-image and embracing your imperfections is vital to becoming at peace with yourself and part of the human experience. As E.E. Cummings noted in the opening quote, self-acceptance in a world that often rewards conformity is a spiritual battle leaving you stronger for having undertaken it. The process requires a healthy dose of compassion, and if you can do it for yourself, you're guaranteed to become a more compassionate person toward others.

BENEFITS OF SELF-COMPASSION

Besides making you a better person, there are tried and true benefits to learning self-compassion; they encompass the physical and mental aspects. Self-compassion comes more naturally to some people. Others have a hard time not beating themselves up over every little thing they've done wrong. It could be a combination of nature and nurture elements. People with very critical parents often find it harder than others to be easier on themselves. Therefore, making an effort to become more forgiving toward yourself is worth it. It gives you valid reasons to teach others how to show compassion.

Possessing strong self-compassion helps you build better health. Not only physical health, but it also ensures your goal setting for relationships and well-being are built on a solid basis. People who know how to exercise self-forgiveness and nurture themselves spiritually are known to have lower anxiety and depression. Since self-compassionate people can better express their pain, they can connect with others deeper and recognize others suffering. When you grant yourself some measure of grace, it becomes easier to recognize when others need the same. So, for people exhibiting self-awareness about their feelings and connecting with others, their emotional well-being is fairly strong, and they are less likely to have various mood disorders. Or, the effects of conditions like depression or anxiety will be less severe and more manageable.

THE DIFFERENCE BETWEEN SELF-ESTEEM AND SELF-COMPASSION

Self-esteem is sometimes used interchangeably with self-compassion, but they're quite different concepts. Self-compassion is stronger than esteem. In layman's terms, self-esteem is the ability to understand your worth and have confidence in your abilities. This way, it is closer to self-respect. Self-compassion is more involved as a concept. In its simplest form, self-compassion is turning compassion inward. You express self-compassion when you can be kind and understanding toward yourself rather than needlessly self-critical. Self-compassion is giving yourself the emotional support you'd offer someone else in your shoes rather than giving them the cold shoulder.

Self-compassion doesn't mean you should let yourself off the hook if you've done something egregious. You must exercise accountability and exhibit responsibility, but you understand what happened and disentangle your motivations. So, you'd expect of yourself precisely what you'd expect of others when they're in a bind or find themselves in a particularly harmful situation.

So, what is the difference between self-compassion and self-esteem? While self-esteem is important, therapists and psychologists actively promote cultivating self-compassion, primarily because self-esteem leans toward narcissism. Most agree this has upended today's culture, making it harder for younger generations to thrive and find their place in the world due to selfishness. So, while feeling confident in yourself and your abilities is an important trait, understanding yourself and others is arguably a better skill to cultivate. Hence, this chapter focuses on self-compassion and uncovering how important it is to ensure you become a well-rounded person.

Before jumping into the exercise section of this chapter, it's best to break down the concept of self-compassion into the three main rubrics, as proposed by major psychologist Dr. Kristin Neff and others:

- **Exhibiting Curiosity Instead of Judging Yourself**

Treating yourself with kindness rather than judging yourself for a mistake means you're more willing to care for yourself and others.

- **Celebrating Humanity Instead of Living in Isolation**

Nobody is perfect. Embracing your imperfections makes you more compassionate and part of the wider human experience. Most people have to work hard to conclude that for themselves, so recognizing it means recognizing that you are part of the same ecosystem.

- **Exercising Mindfulness**

Instead of overthinking an incident, exercising self-compassion means understanding your thoughts and motivations better and understanding whether positive or negative emotions drove you.

Here are a few exercises to help the above feel more tangible and applicable to daily life.

PRACTICING SELF-COMPASSION

You can hone your self-compassion in a few ways. Some provide a quick "pick-me-up," and others help you deepen this skill over time. Here are a few techniques, from the simple to the more involved.

- **Self-Care and the Body**

Comforting your body by listening to it, getting rest, and sleeping well, is one way to practice self-compassion. Unfortunately, the concept of self-care has been commercialized in contemporary culture. However, bringing it back to basics mostly entails prioritizing your health and well-being without spending hundreds of dollars on skincare, for example. So, if you practice simple self-care by eating healthy, resting when needed, walking, or riding a bike, you give yourself a healthy dose of self-compassion.

- **Be a Good Friend to Yourself**

How would you treat people you care about? You would try your hardest to be a good friend. You should do the same for yourself to practice self-compassion. What does this mean? As a friend, you recognize you can't solve all their troubles or take on the entirety of their pain, but you know how to provide emotional support and validate their emotions. So, why not do that for yourself? Be kind to yourself and remember everyone makes mistakes. Don't overthink or over-interpret every action or thought you've ever made or expressed. Rather, you can let things go and acknowledge your humanity in your actions that might not have been precisely what you expected.

When a friend is feeling down, your instinct would be to care for them using body language like a pat on the back or terms of endearment to help buoy them during a tough time. Caring for yourself should be as easy as caring for your friend. So, if you're upset or have been hurt, repeat some mantras in your head and other kind words to help protect you from the pain. The last thing you need is to give a microphone to the overly critical voice in your head that's all too eager to pounce when you've made a mistake.

- ## Think of the Big Picture

When you widen your perspective, you can place problems in the appropriate box and look at them through a more sophisticated prism. It is central to building strong self-compassion. You might be wondering how this works in practice. When you think of the big picture, you will be less invested in getting validation from others. People usually keep themselves busy thinking about how others view them. Social pressure profoundly impacts your psyches. However, focusing your energies elsewhere, how people look at you or your position with a socially ordained hierarchy, becomes less important because your sense of self and happiness is not tied to external forces. Instead, you enact kindness toward yourself.

Another way is reaching out to others when you're having a hard time. It is a way to understand your feelings within a wider context. For example, during the pandemic, even the most introverted people eventually tried to reach out to others to make a connection. It was an exceptionally trying time, and those who felt empowered enough reached out to others to commiserate. These moments helped many survive the upheaval because they realized they weren't alone in their pain. Reaffirming this connectedness helps reframe your problems within a larger context, giving you the confidence to build a social support network and enhancing your well-being.

- ## Become More Mindful

Mindfulness is another way to get out of the doldrums. You can practice mindfulness in several ways. For instance, meditate for a few minutes every day. Depending on how involved you want your practice to be, you can try various forms of meditation. For example, iRest yoga combines the best of yoga with meditation for a more relaxed approach to both practices. Transcendental meditation's benefits have been touted by many. Each is different in how it deals with emotional pain compassionately, extending plenty of kindness to you.

- ## Recount an Experience

If a particular experience that was exceptionally painful sticks out in your mind or causes embarrassment or humiliation, then writing it down might help. You can write about it as part of a journaling exercise or, as some psychologists recommend, write a letter to yourself. This method helps you explain why a particular situation caused you so much consternation without blaming yourself or anyone else. It might sound a bit hokey or something from your basic creative writing class, but exploring your feelings while being kind to yourself is a great exercise. You must shut down the angry, hyper-critical part of yourself to write, which helps develop self-compassion.

- **Practice Affirmations**

Similar to being a good friend to yourself, practicing affirmations is kindness that helps you build a reservoir of self-compassion. Positive affirmations replace self-criticism and are a good way of reminding you to care for yourself.

Examples of positive affirmations you can say to yourself or jot down when going through a rough time are:

- It's ok for me to make mistakes. I forgive myself for them
- I deserve compassion and empathy not only from others but from myself
- My mistakes are an indicator of how much I've grown and continue to learn about myself
- I can ignore how others judge me

Continue to list statements you think would be helpful when you're down and to remind you to love yourself.

- **Let Go of Negative Feelings**

It's sometimes harder than it sounds to be all namaste about life's little indignities. However, holding onto negative feelings won't do you any good. It doesn't mean you should forget when someone has treated you unkindly or be quick to forgive: it simply means to let go so that you don't have corrosive feelings gnawing at you for extended long. You can practice visualization exercises to help you imagine letting go of negative feelings and giving yourself a chance to breathe, let go of the past, and simply be yourself.

• See a Therapist

Seeing a therapist is the ultimate form of self-care and a great way to cultivate a deeper well of self-compassion for yourself. While the idea of seeing a therapist consistently might seem daunting, it's worth reframing your thinking about it. Finding a suitable fit for a therapist is probably the lengthiest part of the process, but there are ways to help blunt this pain. Filter through your search on online websites devoted solely to finding a psychotherapist who accepts your insurance. Book a free consultation with the therapist to determine if you've found the right fit. Another consideration is creating the schedule most comfortable for you with your therapist - there's no need to see them every week if you don't feel it's necessary. Seeing a therapist once a month is a great way to check in with yourself, get a chance to get out of your head, better understand your thought processes, and build your self-confidence. Being mindful is great, but not having a solid sounding board might not be the healthiest way for some people. So, consider seeing a therapist to check on your emotional state and give yourself the space to talk and think out loud.

• Supportive Touch Exercise

Psychotherapist Kristin Neff, who helped pioneer the study of self-compassion, recommends the "supportive touch" exercise as a way to self-soothe. Sometimes giving yourself a hug or reaching for your favorite hot water bottle, you can find comfort when under duress. This is the concept behind this exercise. Different forms of touch help activate the body's "care system," the part of the nervous system allowing you to feel calm and safe. When performing this exercise, leaving your ego or any awkwardness at the door is important: of course, this will seem weird at first, but the focus is to have your body enjoy a sense of comfort. You can add modifications as needed on this exercise as various takes are available. Remember, if needed, you can turn to this exercise a few times a week.

Here are the steps to follow for the Hand on Heart Touch exercise:

1. Take two or three deep, long breaths. This helps to calm your nerves, especially when dealing with more anxiety than usual.

2. Place your hand over your heart, which shouldn't feel too foreign if you've practiced yoga. Focus on the gentle pressure and warm heat emanating from your hand.

3. If you prefer, make small circles with your hand on your chest

4. Next, focus on the rising and falling of your chest as you breathe in and out

5. Continue to focus on your breathing and the feeling of your hand until you feel grounded and calm.

If you've found this helpful, check out other versions of this touch exercise and its relationship to finding calm and quieting anxiety. Undoubtedly, it helps to deepen your self-compassion over time.

COMMON MYTHS

So, a few misconceptions plaguing self-compassion have been indirectly addressed. But there are a few more worth tackling to ensure you understand the positives of cultivating self-compassion better.

A common misnomer of self-compassion is you're giving yourself an excuse. Some people confuse this with never apologizing for engaging in harmful behaviors and language and never practicing accountability. Nothing could be further from the truth. Self-compassionate individuals have stronger empathy and understand how others could have been hurt. They will likely offer a genuine apology and are generally committed to refraining from repeating damaging patterns. For example, psychologists pioneered in this field often point out the extent to which self-compassionate people take part in social justice movements.

Another common mistake people make about self-compassion is confusing the idea with a lack of motivation. To them, it means becoming too comfortable with yourself and never seeing the need for improvement because you accept yourself as you are. Nothing could be further from the truth. Cultivating self-compassion takes a lot of work, leading to tremendous spiritual growth. A self-compassionate person has a realistic outlook on who they are and where they are in life. They can ascertain precisely what is needed to achieve their goals. Considering your limitations as an individual does not equate to a lack of desire to grow - far from it. It means you clearly identify your blind spots and devise a game plan for how to move forward.

KEY TAKEAWAYS

- Practicing self-compassion is not a selfish act, nor does it mean letting yourself off the hook if you've done something particularly erroneous. You remain responsible for your actions but are also given permission to forgive yourself and take lessons from the incident to help you move forward.

- People who cultivate self-compassion are less likely to fall prey to mood disorders like depression or anxiety. Practicing self-compassion can help alleviate the worst symptoms of depression and anxiety in many people and helps ensure overall well-being.

- Positive well-being leads to greater self-confidence in your abilities and more mindfulness and awareness about your actions and their impact on others, making you a more compassionate person.

- Self-compassion is different from self-esteem. Some psychologists place a greater purchase on the former rather than the latter. Cultivating self-esteem doesn't necessarily make you a better person or more aware of how you behave and impact others. Also, when taken to the extreme, it can lead to narcissism and adopting a holier-than-thou attitude, which anyone looking for compassion will find inaccessible or unattractive.

- Self-compassion is a learnable skill. Even those who have grown up in hyper-critical environments can learn to become more compassionate toward themselves and others by quieting their inner critic. It takes practice, and many mindfulness techniques are applicable, but it's a manageable task if you remain committed.

- Self-compassion is a form of self-care. Forget about buying that overpriced face mask unless you really want it. Instead, focus your energies on becoming a more compassionate person toward yourself and others. The exercises listed in this chapter qualify as self-care.

- Practicing self-compassion reminds you of being part of a larger human ecosystem. You cannot look at yourself or your behaviors in a decontextualized way. Furthermore, by reframing your experiences and looking at them through the prism of "the bigger picture," you will be less likely to indulge in self-flagellation whenever something goes wrong. You will see yourself operating from a specific context, within certain parameters, and acknowledge that some things are beyond your control.

Chapter 5

Build Confidence Through Action

"Action is a great restorer and builder of confidence. Inaction is not only the result but the cause of fear."

~Norman Vincent Peale

Whatever your aspirations, you can only become confident in achieving them if you take the first step. Often, taking action means stepping out of your comfort zone, which is challenging, hence, why people shy away from it. However, you can't gain momentum to make the changes you desire without putting the necessary effort into action.

This chapter focuses on the transformative power of actionable steps, highlighting the value of learning through action. It teaches you the importance of trying several times, if necessary, regardless of the outcome. Through practical exercises and real-life examples, it helps you learn to view challenges and setbacks as opportunities for learning and improvement, engage in new experiences, and celebrate your bravery and progress.

UNDERSTAND THE CONNECTION BETWEEN CONFIDENCE AND ACTION

Have you ever wondered what sets apart successful women from those who couldn't achieve their dreams? The former took action, but the latter didn't. Now you might wonder, "How can I take action if I lack confidence? It is a valid concern. However, contrary to popular belief, it's the action that fosters confidence, not the other way around. You must act before you become confident to act. In turn, you become even more confident and continue the cycle of confidence.

Regardless of how much you lack confidence in your ability to achieve something, you must take the first step. You won't be confident enough before taking the first step, making waiting for your confidence to emerge futile. However, taking that crucial first step will make you feel more competent. You might hesitate to take action because you didn't believe you were good enough to achieve your goals. Whether embarking on a new profession, starting a business, or another venture, doubting yourself can hinder you from trying. Taking action will make you feel empowered. You'll see that while you don't know whether your first step is the right one, it doesn't matter. You can always start again or figure things out on the go. No matter how little experience you have, taking action will make you feel more confident and allow you to learn more.

According to research published in *Nature Communications*, neuroplasticity is crucial in linking action and confidence. Scientists compared the brain scans of a group of people and found that some had brain activity patterns associated with high self-confidence. Others' activity patterns reflected low self-confidence. The group was then subjected to an activity-based training session devised to raise their confidence – only the participants weren't aware of this specific goal. Despite this, researchers found that the brains of those with low confidence adopted new patterns. Consequently, their confidence soared.

Competence fosters self-belief. Once you take action and feel competent, your thought will change from "I can't do this" and "I don't know how to do this" to "I can do it" and "I will learn to get better at this." As you invest more time working on your goal, you continually boost and prove your competence, further fueling your self-confidence. You become confident in what you're doing, realize you're good at it, and the results validate this belief. As your confidence soars, you channel it back into the action. You're continuing the momentum because you feel it's worth it. You're making a change confidently without worrying your efforts will be hindered.

FIGURE OUT WHAT PREVENTS YOU FROM TAK-ING ACTION

Now that you know the importance of taking action to boost your confidence, it's time to consider what's preventing you from taking action. There could be several reasons you refuse to take that critical first step. Here are a few common ones:

- **Lack of time:** This often stems from improper prioritization. As soon as you prioritize productive habits, you'll notice you have far more time to work on that first step.

- **Procrastination:** This goes hand in hand with your failure to prioritize conducive habits. Learn why you do it in the first place and address those issues to avoid procrastination.

- **Fear of judgment or criticism:** You might fear what others think if you decide to change. Or worse, you might be terrified to face your inner critic - that little negative voice judging your every action. Letting go of your fears can free you from their paralyzing effects and get you moving in the right direction.

- **Lack of clarity:** If you aren't sure how to start taking action, you aren't alone. Very few people began their plans with specific ideas on where to start. Most start with nothing, making it even sweeter when they achieve something.

CONSIDER WHAT TAKING ACTION MEANS TO YOU

Another crucial step in overcoming the mentioned roadblocks is to consider what taking action means to you. Is taking action to build confidence in a specific aspect of life what you want? What's it worth to you to become good at where you lack confidence? These questions might cause discomfort, but that's the point of this contemplative exercise. Being confronted with your weaknesses can be daunting, but it's crucial for growth because it makes you step out of your comfort zone. When you find the answer, you'll know where to start.

Understand What You Want

Being clear about what you want gives you purpose, drive, and plenty of confidence. The following testimony is a great example:

"My friend Claire and I wanted to set up a vacation fund. Claire didn't know when or where she wanted to go on vacation or how big a fund, she would need to make this possible. However, I have worked out a detailed plan for when I wanted to take my holiday and what money I needed to save by this date. This plan included money for emergencies and fun activities. This plan made me feel confident to raise enough money for my vacation and gave me the driving force to achieve this goal. I saved enough money in time, while my friend had to work much longer, and she still had cash flow issues when on vacation. It was because she wasn't confident enough and didn't have the foresight to contemplate what she wanted." – Lilly

Stop Being Afraid

Most people who lack confidence tiptoe through life, hoping to avoid negative emotions. However, being afraid to take action means you're doing yourself a disservice because you'll never avoid feeling negative emotions. Life is full of ups and downs, and feeling bad on occasion is inevitable. Stop being afraid to take action and consider the possibility of having a positive experience. More often than not, you'll enjoy taking the first step. If you succeed, you'll see a boost in your confidence. If you don't, you can always try something new. After all, the worse that can happen is you feeling poorly, which you'll survive. So, stop tiptoeing through life and take that first actionable step.

Push Your Boundaries

Being afraid to step out of your comfort zone will make you hesitate to manifest changes. Push the boundaries you're comfortable with, and you'll see your confidence soar. For instance, you want to take on more responsibility in school projects but are afraid to ask your teacher about it. You've become comfortable with the tasks you're always assigned and don't want to risk trying something new. You've probably gone out of your way to avoid getting considered for a different role. The trick is to start with small steps. Perhaps, you can chime in with a few constructive ideas at the next meeting to show your teacher you can do more. Then, ask for responsibilities, like presenting on behalf of your team at the next meeting. Once you start doing this, you'll notice your self-confidence rising. You might notice you're no longer uncomfortable doing something different and enjoy your new responsibilities. Your teacher will also notice your change, raising the likelihood of more growth opportunities.

Establish Positive Habits

Positive habits keep your physical, mental, and emotional health in check, boosting your confidence. A positive habit makes you feel empowered and happy, from a balanced diet to nurturing your mind with knowledge to volunteering. Mindfulness exercises can be a fantastic habit to increase your confidence, and so is moving your body. Regular physical activity can boost your self-esteem for several reasons. Moving your body improves blood and oxygen flow through your organs, energizing and helping you focus. Likewise, getting enough sleep will go a long way, boosting your productivity and confidence. Physical activity and adequate sleep enable you to unwind and process your stressors.

It takes time and determination to incorporate positive habits into your life. However, dedicating 30 minutes a day is better than not doing anything at all. It will all be worth it once you notice how it affects your confidence.

Eliminate Negative Thoughts

Negative thinking is a self-limiting habit. For example, you might think you're an unsociable person after a one-time embarrassing moment at a party. You think you're awkward and can't talk to anyone, so you avoid social events. When you must attend them, you're shy when attempting to interact with people and remain silent, even though you could contribute to the conversation. Learning to identify and avoid these negative thoughts is a powerful action.

Take Smaller Steps

Taking action won't seem so intimidating when taking smaller steps. For example, if your idea for taking action is a goal to buy a new computer, don't focus on this. If you do, and forever calculating how much you have to save for it, you'll likely struggle to achieve this goal. Break it into smaller goals, like saving a small amount of money every week and putting it aside to avoid being overwhelmed. Small, achievable goals will significantly improve your confidence to achieve your goal and buy a new computer.

Involve Others

It is much easier to achieve anything substantial with a support system. Knowing you have friends and family to rely on will make you believe anything is possible. An action step could be to reach out to others. However, a word to the wise, consider only people who will support your goals and dreams; they'll help you achieve them. If they don't, they're likely to hinder your success. Delegate your tasks if needed. All successful women surround themselves with a support system.

However, if you feel more empowered to start a venture on your own, do it. It can be liberating to do it alone. It will motivate and raise your confidence in conquering obstacles and milestones. Yet, if things become too hard, it's time to realize you can only do so much yourself.

Consider Helping Others

Showing kindness is another way to involve others in taking action to raise confidence. Give back to your community by helping those in need. It will remind you of your values and motivate you to do more than you thought possible. The benefits will arise instantaneously. Even doing something as small as donating your time to a local charity will make you feel more productive. Charitable activities foster creativity, allowing you to find unorthodox but effective solutions to problems. Focusing on other people's needs will boost your strength when you're exhausted. After a while, you'll notice a surge in your confidence if you use your time and skills to help others.

Learn to Manage Your Time

As you've surmised from the beginning of the chapter, managing your time is crucial for productive actions. How many times have you been caught up in a heap of tasks and stressed because of bad time management skills? Whatever the number is, you aren't alone. Time management is a learned skill, and learning to get everything done takes time. However, once you do, you'll feel more competent and confident in taking charge of your life.

Time management doesn't have to be complicated. You can do it through simple actions, like making a to-do list at the beginning of the day. You can do this in 10 minutes and take another 10 to sort out the tasks based on their order of importance. Now you can tackle the chores or assignments, beginning with the most pressing item on the list.

Celebrate Your Achievements

Celebrate your accomplishments to keep positive and motivated. Don't just put them out of your mind and move on to the new one as soon as you finish them. Acknowledging your achievements is powerful action guaranteed to inspire you when setting future goals. Knowing you'll get to celebrate gives you something to look forward to and render goal-achieving fun.

Give yourself small rewards after every achievement. For small ones, these could be taking a short trip. For larger ones, buy yourself something you wanted for a long time. It will make a substantial difference in your ability to achieve your goals. With a reward in front of you, you will be more likely to find the energy and drive to accomplish your goals. Moreover, your confidence will grow with each reward obtained.

Don't be limited to large achievements. Appreciate small wins, too. Another reason to break large actionable steps into smaller ones is it enables you to get more confidence-boosting rewards.

Practice Gratitude

Another great way to raise your confidence through action is by practicing gratitude. You'll be more confident in yourself if you take your time to acknowledge and appreciate the positives in your life. Whether it's people who positively influenced your growth or something you were lucky enough to have in your life, allow yourself to feel grateful for it. Alternatively, compose a list of what you're thankful for at the end of each day. Focus on what made you happy or confident during the day. After finishing it, read over the list.

You could make a more comprehensive list of general experiences; this time includes negative ones. Remember, they helped shape who you are just as positive ones did. Don't be ashamed of your failures, or let them control you. Take action to approach what caused you to fail more confidently. The outcome will soon change.

Visualize Your Goals

Besides planning what you want to achieve, keep a visual reminder of your goal. For example, a vision board with pictures and descriptor words for the ideal outcome lets you imagine your future success and make bold decisions. Alternatively, visualize your goal. For instance, if you want to be admitted to a sports team, see yourself playing on the team. It's a powerful action guaranteed to boost your confidence during tryouts.

Another fantastic goal to visualize is shifting your self-image. As a crucial aspect of your life, your self-image might be hindering you from becoming a more confident version of yourself. If you have a mental picture of yourself lacking confidence, visualize changing it. Consider why you have that image and what you can do to fix it. Do you think less of yourself because you made a mistake in the past? Visualize yourself going through the same experience without making a mistake. Your self-image will shift automatically.

Start Acting Confidently

Did you know you can manifest confidence by acting confidently? For instance, you feel awkward talking to others at social events. Taking small actions like speaking more slowly and straightening your posture will make you look more confident. Do you wish you had the confidence to say no when saying yes means your needs won't be met? If your friends and family can easily talk you into doing favors for them, it's up to you to change this habit. The best course of action is to set firm boundaries and make them respected. Practice polite rejections so that you'll have the power to say no the next time your friend hits you up for a little favor when you're already busy juggling a million tasks.

Realize You're Equal to Others

Girls are afraid to take action because they're conditioned to belittle themselves. Instead of learning true self-knowledge, you might have been taught to compare yourself to others. For example, you might have been compared to a sibling, friend, or relative of a similar age with better grades, was more polite, had nicer hair, etc. Over time, you adapted this thinking. However, you must change this habit to boost your confidence and stop comparing yourself to those around you. After all, no one starts with beaming confidence. Everyone had to recognize and value their potential at some point. You should do the same. Accepting you're as worthy of success as everyone else is another action for building self-confidence.

KEY TAKEAWAYS

- Understanding how taking action begets confidence is crucial for self-improvement
- Once you see the benefits of taking action, the next move is to contemplate what's preventing you from taking the first step and what taking action means to you
- Gaining better insight into what you want to achieve empowers you to push your boundaries and take the first step, regardless of how uncomfortable it makes you feel
- Establishing positive habits and reducing negative ones to a minimum goes a long way in converting dreams into action
- Likewise, involving others (whether for their support or helping them) is a good avenue for boosting confidence through action
- You're afraid to say no. Learning to say no is a critical action when prioritizing your needs
- Learning to manage your time cuts down on procrastination and excuses for not taking action. Becoming productive makes you feel more confident in what you do
- Cutting down bigger steps into manageable portions makes the prospect of taking action less daunting
- Don't forget to celebrate your successes, including the small victories. They're equally fundamental in life-changing and confidence-boosting actions
- Practice gratitude, even for bad experiences. These could be fantastic learning opportunities, so you should be grateful for them
- Visualize your goals and act according to your vision. The results will come sooner than you think, boosting your self-confidence
- Understand you're equal to everyone else. No one is born with high confidence. Everyone had to build confidence, and one of their first moves was to take action.

Chapter 6

Embracing Failure as Growth

"Our greatest weakness lies in giving up. The most certain way to succeed is always to try just one more time."

- Thomas A. Edison

Failure is an imminent and necessary part of life. However, how you counter it can immensely affect your growth and development as a person. Instead of considering failure as proof of your incompetence, lack of veritable skills, or poor luck, you can use well-tried cognitive techniques called framing and reframing to embrace it as a learning opportunity. Reading this chapter, you will understand the importance of reframing your failures into invaluable lessons, how to do it, and how other women have done it successfully.

WHAT IS FAILURE?

Failure is a monumental opportunity to reflect on what went wrong, identify weak areas of your character and skillsets, and obtain new perspectives. Embracing failure means acknowledging its value rather than fearing or hiding from it.

Here is a quick rundown of the benefits you can gain by embracing failure:

- **Personal growth:** Failure can test your boundaries and foster growth. Anytime you fail, you can reflect on your goals, beliefs, and values and establish new ones if needed. Embracing failure motivates you to take risks and pursue new challenges, shaping your personality.

- **Enhanced problem-solving skills:** If you want to overcome your failures, you must reflect on what went wrong and devise an alternative solution. As you do, you hone your problem-solving and critical-thinking skills. By acknowledging your mistakes, you made the first step in developing more effective problem-solving, lowering your chances of future failures.

- **Improved resilience:** Embracing your mistakes makes you resilient. It empowers you to overcome setbacks and continue pursuing the same or different goals. As you become more resilient, you learn to view failure as a natural part of learning, creating a productive cycle for better decision-making.

- **Higher confidence:** Gaining confidence goes hand in hand with embracing failure. Embracing and circumventing defeat gains you the confidence to pursue new challenges with an empowered, positive attitude.

WHAT IS REFRAMING?

Reframing is the change of the frame (view) you create about present situations. Your frame is based on your core beliefs, expectations, emotions, and learned ideas. During reframing, you adopt a different viewpoint. Besides finding a new meaning for an outcome or situation, reframing can also lead to discovering positive aspects. For instance, if you fail a test, you might initially frame this as a disaster because it lowers your average. Then, as you start reframing it, you learn to see your test result as feedback on skills you need to improve.

Are you wondering why framing and reframing are crucial for confidence building? How you see defeat can dampen or boost your motivation and resilience and, in turn, your self-confidence. By framing your failures unhealthily, you become ashamed, discouraged, and unmotivated to take on new experiences. In contrast, if you view your mistakes positively, you become hopeful, encouraged, and curious to seek new challenges. It will boost the skills needed to fare in stressful and frustrating circumstances and foster a growth mindset motivating you to peruse your mistakes and learn from them. As soon as you view failures as lessons instead of punishment, your thought patterns become more positive instantly, fostering curiosity and drive.

A FEW STORIES TO INSPIRE YOU TO EMBRACE FAILURE

Failing in a relationship can be incredibly difficult. However, as you'll see from the following testimony, there are always lessons to be learned.

"I married young but was very happy, which is why my divorce hit hard. At first, I was frantically trying to make it work purely because the idea of getting divorced felt embarrassing. I didn't want to let my family down, and for the same reason, it took me a while to move on. I was mourning the idea of a happy life I thought I had beforehand, so I took my time with it.

I must say, despite the hardships, I wouldn't change things about this period. The only thing I would say to my younger self is that you can live again after divorce because, at the time, it felt like the end of the world. After a while, I realized that my marriage wasn't working, and if something fails, it's better to let it go than to cling to something that makes you stressed. I have so much to live for, and life is too short to spend it being afraid of making mistakes.

Now I embrace failure, and I can say I even expect it without trepidation. I accept that life has a learning curve, and wisdom that comes from missteps makes it all worthwhile. Failing is uncomfortable, making it challenging to accept. However, once I learned to step out of my comfort zone, I could challenge myself in ways I never thought possible.

I advise any woman in the same position to get to the deep root of her feelings about their missteps and defeats. Ask yourself - what's the worst that would happen if you did make a mistake? When was the first time you felt like a failure? How did it make you feel deep inside? Allow yourself to fail because it's the only way you can grow. Remember, you're the only one standing in the way of your happiness." - Isabelle

As the following example illustrates, failing on a professional level can be as difficult yet as instructive as a personal life failure:

"I worked as a financial manager at a bank overseeing a project that went terribly wrong. None of the data was properly collected, our superiors were livid, and none of my team members would do their jobs. Every day for several weeks, I gave my best to pick up the slack after them and make the project I was responsible for work, somehow. Day after day, I was trying to resolve more and more issues, sometimes bringing myself to the edge of tears due to the stress because I didn't feel I had a choice. Unfortunately, it wasn't enough because I couldn't stop the project from going up in flames. I learned a lot about accountability from this experience.

Do you know what else I learned? I wasn't equipped to deal with those project types, and they're best left in the hands of people with more experience in the industry. I quit my job and became a real estate agent - a similar multitasking job, but much better suited to my skills and personality traits. I had several other failures, and each one taught me resilience. They taught me that failing is not the end of the world.

I wouldn't say I'm completely at peace with defeat - it still hurts when I fail at something. However, I've learned what it is to expect failure - especially when focusing on big goals than to let them catch you by surprise. One of my core values is that I can push myself outside my comfort zone and anticipate that my projects might fail." - Maggie

Lastly, here is a testimony about embracing failure in different aspects of life:

"I learned not to berate myself over defeats. When I fail, I have a nice conversation with myself as I would with a friend experiencing a hardship. I try to be compassionate and supportive. What I never do is tell myself I am useless. Failure is a true eye-opener. Give yourself an hour of lamenting your defeat if you must, then switch gears and try again.

I learned this lesson when I wanted to start an online blog about healthy nutrition and the benefits of organic food. However, my attempt failed because I partnered with somebody with different goals. They had a background in web design and were supposed to teach me the skills to manage the blog. In the meantime, I was utilizing my voice on social media to raise awareness about the importance of healthy nutrition for women and its impact on their lives as mothers, friends, daughters, partners, and professionals. It was an honor that I could spread the word, and women were receptive to it. I wanted to utilize my voice to launch this big project, but it was too much for me and my partner to handle.

So, I failed to launch my blog. However, instead of despairing, I saw it as a redirection. I needed to focus more on teaching about healthy nutrition like I was originally doing on social media. The evidence was the messages from women across the country on my social media: "It was so great seeing somebody who helps us learn about the value of nutrition and organic food."

So, the way I see it, while I didn't accomplish my original goal, I didn't fail either. I realize now that my failure was a lesson to learn from, and I made peace with it. I learned that sometimes, we have to reevaluate the route we take toward our goals. The image I conceived of my dreams, goals, and inspiration might look vastly different than it did in the beginning. However, my core values are unchanged, and that's what truly matters. I moved on by accepting that I didn't reach my target in the original format, and it's okay because it enabled me to pave a different way (an even better one) to manifest my dreams. I just needed to take the time to reevaluate my goals. If anything, it was a misdirection on my part rather than a defeat, and all I needed to do was reroute.

My failure taught me that you don't always have to achieve something new or expected. I needed to focus on what I was doing already. Nowadays, I am positively at peace with failing because I know I can't succeed at everything. Otherwise, what would motivate me to hone my skills and develop new ones? I am thankful for all my defeats and the insights I gained from them. They taught me how to honor my beliefs and values. I am comfortable with failure because it often allows me to do something new.

Your perception makes a vast difference in seeing something as a defeat or a learning prospect. Appreciate what you couldn't accomplish because those experiences weren't in vain. They gave you something even if it wasn't something you expected to gain. They gave you knowledge." - Laura

PRACTICAL TIPS TO OVERCOME FEAR OF FAILURE

Now that you've read these inspiring stories, you might feel more encouraged to learn about the best techniques for overcoming a fear of failure.

Understand That You Could Know Success Only If You Failed Beforehand

The most eye-opening perspective on success is gained through the mistakes you make along the way. Assumptions and solutions are fundamental for success. You must accept that some assumptions don't work, and if you fail, your assumption is probably faulty. Every failed attempt teaches you what works. Failure gives you perspective. It helps you focus and hone in on the right solutions.

In other words, failing could mean you made assumptions that did not work. Had you not failed, you wouldn't know this, so it is a great lesson. Honor your failures and acknowledge the valuable lessons they provide. It's also a good idea to record your mistakes and the lessons you learned from them. Over time, you will see how far you have come and how much you have grown.

Grasp the Learning Process

Take on the learning journey and failure as a crucial part of the process. During this journey, reflect on what went wrong, what you could have done differently, and what you can deduce from the experience to gain valuable insights and improve.

Mistakes are the imperfections that push us toward perfection. However, they can only become mistakes if you don't learn from them. If you do, they're not mistakes but life lessons. After a mistake, carefully review every step to determine what didn't work. Learning from your mistakes will make you successful on the next attempt. You can view failures as warm-up exercises devised to help you become better at what you do.

Use the insight you learned from the failed opportunities by taking action. Think about what you can do to improve and move forward. Whether delving into the same venture again or pursuing a new route, taking action will help you grow and develop as a person.

Have a Supportive Network

Surround yourself with a network of friends and family who support you as your work toward your dreams. The more people you have to encourage and motivate you, the better. A support system can take a load off your shoulders when you must embrace failure. It enables you to stay motivated and focused on your goals.

Boost Your Mental Fitness

As you start looking at failure as a learning journey, you'll discover plenty of opportunities for improving yourself. Adding tools to your success ensures the toolbox is picking up new skills. Alternatively, hone the existing ones. Set up a mental fitness plan by incorporating it into your journey. You're raising your chances of success with increased cognitive abilities like memory recall and critical thinking.

Push the Fear Back

Sometimes the fear of failure masks a hidden fear of success. Big successes require work, time, and effort, not to mention stepping out of your comfort zone. The success might challenge conventional wisdom and socially accepted norms, which can be intimidating. Don't be afraid to say no to the fear and push it to the back of your mind. The insights you gain from your mistakes will occupy plenty of mind space to achieve this.

Understand That Success Is Always Built on Failures

With big dreams come big failures. However, big failures don't mean you won't achieve your dreams. Embrace your big failures as valuable lessons to learn from. Understand that the more substantial you fail, the closer you are to your goal; this can be a particularly painful pill to swallow, but don't let it limit you. You must push yourself harder the next time, and you'll overcome your obstacles. Whereas if you let it limit you, you create more hurdles. Don't be afraid to dream big or to experience big failures - they lead to big successes.

Use Your Failure to Unlock Your Creative Side

Life is full of experimenting and failing. You might repeatedly fail in your endeavors, just as many successful women did before obtaining their goals. Many creations in this world wouldn't exist if people accepted that failure is the end of the road. However, they found more creative solutions and succeeded because they chose to circumvent the issue. Sometimes you have to think outside the box to achieve success.

See Failure as Success in Progress

Sometimes you will think you've failed when you're still getting there. In reality, this is only a sign that you must think and work harder, and be more persistent. When working toward a large goal, it's useful to see failure as a temporary delay, not a defeat. It is a matter of finding the right solution for every problem. The recipe to success has several ingredients, and temporary setbacks are merely one of them. You must learn to use these ingredients and combine them with others. For example, conjoining a lesson you learned from your mistakes with a growth mindset results in effective ingredients in attractive packaging. Timing is also key. If you think you've failed, try again later.

Never Give Up

A failure always stings, and typically you want to throw in the towel. Except, you shouldn't. Be persistent in pursuit of your dreams. It might take some reframing of perspectives. For example, can you break your big goal into little wins? The idea of tackling a big project or task you've already failed or feel you'll fail seems extremely daunting. It makes you abandon your ideas repeatedly.

In contrast, by setting smaller goals, you keep motivated and prevent yourself from giving up. If you recently failed at something, give yourself a moment to process it, feel the emotions, and then reframe the perceived failure as an opportunity for growth. Contemplate what you've learned from your mistakes instead of giving up.

KEY TAKEAWAYS

- No one likes to fail, but it happens to everybody. Those who embrace their mistakes as growth opportunities are more confident and likely to succeed

- Reframing negative aspects of failure from positive viewpoints goes a long way in overcoming the fear of failure

- Failure can hit hard in all aspects of life, but it's up to you to work through it and convert it into a lesson well-learned

- Push the fear to the back of your mind by filling your mind with constructive thoughts you can learn from

- Embrace the learning opportunity and use the insights you gained to avoid making the same mistakes

- Surrounding yourself with supportive individuals is another way to become more confident in your ability to succeed

- Boosting your cognitive skills and unlocking your creativity will do wonders for overcoming the fear of failure

- You can't expect to succeed without failure. Every successful woman failed at one point or another. Without this exercise, they wouldn't be where they are now

- Another way to refrain from the negativity of failure is to view it as a success in progress. You didn't fail, you merely found how not to succeed, but your journey toward success continues

- Lastly, don't give up. Pursuing your goals after failure (or despite the fear of failure), you grow as a person

Chapter 7

Assertiveness and Effective Communication

"A strong woman understands that gifts such as logic, decisiveness, and strength are just as feminine as intuition and emotional connection. She values and uses all of her gifts."

- Nancy Rathburn

Even today, women continue to be underrated, underappreciated, and expected to accommodate other people's needs over their own. Women are generally less assertive than men and find it challenging to communicate their needs and wants to others. It can be attributed to the deep-rooted norms and stereotypes ingrained into their brains from an early age. Historically, women have been given roles concerning nurturing and caregiving, while men have always been expected to be assertive and dominant. These gender norms have shaped expectations and behaviors for centuries that women should be submissive and more accommodating than men.

Even today, when feminism is at its peak, many women, especially young girls, find it hard to speak out for their rights. When they do speak out, they're often met with skepticism, resistance, or hostility in some cases, making them want to never be assertive again. However, to succeed in life and accomplish your goals, you must learn to be assertive. What does the term "assertive" mean? The Cambridge Dictionary defines assertiveness as "behaving confidently and being able to say what you want or believe directly."

You want assertiveness in every aspect of your life, whether your career or relationships. You'll never achieve your goals and fulfill your desires if you let people walk all over you. Today, one of the most debated topics about gender equality is women experience biases in many aspects of their careers and are often paid less than their male counterparts. However, you must find your voice and be assertive to break the glass ceiling and receive equal treatment. When you decide to go after what you want, stand up for what you believe in, and push for the change you'd like to see in this world, you'd be surprised at what you can achieve with this attitude.

Unfortunately, many young girls lose their voice and confidence when they hit puberty because of various self-esteem issues and the societal need to adhere to the stereotypical feminine ideal. The world expects girls to be gentle and delicate; however, these characteristics are not realistic of how women are. If a woman deviates even a little from their so-called feminine definition, society labels her a rebel or a bitch. Most women who are assertive about their needs and wants are instantly classified as a bitch, or a rude person.

Moreover, women are expected to resolve tensions instead of exacerbating a situation. This belief prevents them from exercising their agency, voice, and independence. Women are expected to keep the peace by staying quiet and not voicing their opinions. Many women have to endure this daily, compulsively resolving emotional tensions in every situation. For instance, they apologize for every little thing, even when they haven't done anything wrong. They feel compelled to keep a cheerful and happy demeanor no matter what they're going through. They feel they have to always take the high road in a relationship or be the bigger person in fights. They often have to hear, "Boys will be boys," and are expected to accept that as an explanation for their unruly behavior. Many women are so accommodating that after a while, they forget to consider their preferences before anyone else's.

So, how can you be assertive without being rude? How do you get rid of your natural tendency to accommodate the needs of others? How can you communicate your feelings, needs, and wants to others, be it your partner, parents, coworkers, or boss? These are covered in this chapter about assertiveness and communicating as a woman.

You will learn to navigate every life situation easily through the many role-playing exercises provided in this chapter.

STOP PEOPLE-PLEASING

Although people-pleasing is a habit men and women have, women have a higher tendency to put others' needs before theirs and find it hard to say no. Many women resort to people-pleasing because of their low self-esteem issues and want to make others like them. If you find yourself agreeing with people about things you don't agree with, you might be a people-pleaser. This inherent need to please others can be extremely hard to shake off because women are hardwired to compromise on their needs if it helps others. However, this habit only creates problems for you and makes other people take advantage of you. Unfortunately, most women are so used to people-pleasing that they have no idea they're doing it. For them, this behavior is normal, or "being helpful," even if they're inconvenienced by it.

If you're in denial about your people-pleasing habits, here are some sure signs you're a pushover person:

1. You're Inconvenienced

If you're someone who says yes to any favor, even if they inconvenience you, then you're a people-pleaser or a yes-woman. You might not consider your priorities while going out of your way to help others. For instance, you and your friends are trying to decide on a restaurant to go to, and everyone else expresses a preference for a cuisine you don't particularly enjoy. Instead of voicing your opinion, you remain silent and go along with the majority to avoid conflict or seem "difficult." This is a textbook example of a people-pleaser.

2. You Create an Expectation

When you always say "yes" to every favor, the people around you will take you for granted. So, instead of asking you before they make a decision, they'll simply inform you the next time. As a result, the favors you are doing will quickly turn into obligations, becoming even more difficult to get out of them. Some people might become incredibly entitled and expect you to help them no matter what. For instance, your neighbors know you rarely say "no" when they ask for small favors, like picking up groceries or walking their pets. As a result, they will expect you to help them out regularly.

3. You Have a Low Opinion of Yourself

The main problem with people-pleasers is they have a very low opinion of themselves. As a result, their self-worth becomes dependent on other people's validation, so they go out of their way to make others happy. If you feel you're not a good person when you can't help someone, then you're a people-pleaser. You should know it is not your job to give favors and help everyone. Prioritizing your needs does not make you a bad person. You shouldn't have to worry about others not liking you.

4. You Can't Say No

When someone asks you for help, you can't imagine saying no. You knowingly say yes to every favor, aware that you cannot fulfill your needs while helping others with their problems. For instance, your partner frequently requests small favors, like running errands or doing their chores. While these requests pile up, you find it hard to say no, because you don't want to upset your partner.

5. You Apologize or Accept Fault Even When You're Not at Fault

As a people-pleaser, you might have the tendency to apologize readily, even when you're not at fault. If you're the one always saying sorry for everything, the problem is with you. For instance, maybe you lend your friend a book, and they misplace it. Instead of holding them accountable for the lost book, you apologize for lending it in the first place, taking the blame.

6. Conflicts Upset You

Maybe this is due to childhood trauma, but most people-pleasers avoid conflicts like the plague. They're scared to be confronted by people and to confront people. As a result, they do anything and everything to diffuse the tension, like taking the blame or saying yes to unreasonable demands. For instance, you're uncomfortable with a friend's behavior but can't bring yourself to confront them, so you say nothing and pretend everything is okay.

7. You're the Giver

You're known as the giver of the group. You're helpful to everyone, even when it's not feasible. Most importantly, you do it so others will like you more and prefer your company. You do this so others will reciprocate with love and affection. However, this creates a vicious cycle in the long run. You'll find yourself "giving" until you burn out, and there's nothing left. When that happens, everyone will make you the villain because of the expectations you've set yourself by always saying yes.

8. You're Afraid of Hurting Other People's Feelings

As a people-pleaser, you hate to hurt someone else's feelings or cause them trouble. So, you bend over backward to help them, even if it hurts your feelings. Although it's not wrong to help people and be there for them, you must draw the line somewhere. Your feelings are as important as other people's. When, despite your financial strain, you lend money to a friend because you're afraid of hurting their feelings, you're inevitably hurting yourself.

9. You Have No Free Time

Take a good look at your schedule. Is it packed with things you've promised to do for others? While being busy doesn't make you a people-pleaser, a jam-packed schedule where you're mostly doing favors for others is a sign you're stretching yourself thin to help others. Think of the last time you did something for yourself. If you can't think of an occasion to have some good old-fashioned "me-time," then you're taking on more than you can handle.

The question begs, how do you stop being a people-pleaser and start making time for yourself? The answer is by being assertive. When you set boundaries assertively, people won't come asking for unreasonable favors. Even if they do, you'll have the guts to say no.

ASSERTIVENESS, AGGRESSIVENESS, AND PASSIVENESS

"To be passive is to let others decide for you. To be aggressive is to decide for others. To be assertive is to decide for yourself." - Edith Eva Eger

Before you can incorporate assertiveness into your lifestyle, you must understand the difference between being passive, aggressive, and assertive. Many people confuse assertiveness with aggressiveness and ultimately ruin many relationships.

Passive

Passive behavior coincides with people-pleasing behavior. If you cannot say no, and later feel overwhelmed and helpless, you act as the passive party. You might not realize it, but you advertise your passive status through certain behaviors and demeanors. For instance, if you have a meek voice, avoid eye contact, or hover in the background, people will seek you out for help because they believe they can push you to do anything.

Aggressive

On the other hand, aggressive behavior uses violence, force, or intimidation to get what you want. The aggression doesn't have to be physical; simple mental intimidation is enough to convince someone. As long as they're afraid, you have power over them. It's quite common to transition from being assertive to being aggressive, which is not a good decision. When you attempt to be assertive, you express your needs and boundaries confidently. However, certain behaviors or communication styles might unintentionally come across as aggressive.

Passive Aggressive

Back in the day, dealing with people was pretty straightforward - you had three behavior types to think about; passive, aggressive, and assertive. But things have gotten more complicated now, and an increasing "passive-aggressive" behavior is exhibited. These people indirectly throw shade and manipulate situations to get what they want. Picture those coworkers who intentionally mess up, hoping you'll pick up their slack. Or those who always show up late, leaving you to cover for them. These people use sarcastic remarks or backhanded compliments to criticize or mock others without directly confronting the issue.

Assertive

Being assertive means thinking independently, confidently, and self-assuredly and standing up for yourself. As an assertive person, you act in your best interest and tell others how you feel without sounding rude or obnoxious. You are honest, direct, respectful, thoughtful, confident, and firm about your decisions. Assertiveness includes speaking clearly and concisely to get your message across. An assertive person is not conscious of themselves and has a confident demeanor, automatically letting others know they can't be bullied or forced into doing something they don't want to do.

SETTING BOUNDARIES

A huge part of being assertive is setting clear boundaries. It is communicating your limits, needs, and expectations to others clearly and respectfully. Setting boundaries establishes guidelines for how you want to be treated, what you're willing to tolerate, and what is essential for your well-being.

Consider these tips when setting boundaries:

Take a Good Look Back

The first step to setting healthy boundaries is reflecting on past experiences and considering how you felt in specific situations. Contemplate the moments that stand out to you. For instance, think about the last time you had to finish all the dishes or were pressured into going to a party. Or instances when you were the one to complete a group project. Here's an exercise to help you get started. Grab a pen and paper, and jot down how you felt in each situation you've encountered. For example:

- "I don't feel comfortable when my coworkers ask me about my childhood"
- "I don't feel comfortable being set up by my friends for a date"
- "I feel angry whenever I'm made to close up the shop alone by my coworkers"
- "I feel resentful whenever my partner refuses to do the dishes and waits for me to do them"

Keep adding to the list over time. It creates a basic framework for your boundaries, making it clear when someone might be crossing a line. Remember, boundaries are flexible in certain situations, but you should know when to differentiate between what's logical and when you feel you're being pushed into it.

QUESTIONS TO ASK YOURSELF WHEN SETTING BOUNDARIES

Using past experiences is a great way to set boundaries for the future. For example, if Situation A made you uncomfortable before, jot it down in your notebook. Later, when a similar situation arises, you'll have a solid reference to decide on. But what if you're facing Situation A for the first time? No worries. You can create an evaluation plan to help you decide whether to do it.

Here are some guide questions for setting new boundaries:

- How do you feel about the action? If it doesn't sit well with you, then it's best to avoid it altogether.
- Do you have other important things to do? Consider your schedule. Don't forget to prioritize self-care. Everyone needs a mental health day, and postponing it for someone else could lead to burnout later.
- What's the nature of the request? Is it genuine or a frivolous favor? Assess the person's needs and intentions before committing.
- Is their need greater than yours? Weigh it out - your needs versus theirs. Building self-esteem helps you decide fairly instead of always putting others' needs before yours.
- How will helping them make you feel? Instead of feeling bad for refusing help, consider how you'll feel if you do help. Will it make you feel good and appreciated, or is it just the usual routine?

Remember, these questions are handy when dealing with requests. Since each situation is different, your decision-making will naturally change accordingly. So, trust yourself and find a balance between helping others and caring for yourself.

TYPES OF BOUNDARIES

1. Physical Boundaries

These should be about respecting your personal space. It might sound simple, but setting these boundaries can be challenging once they're crossed. For instance, do you prefer hugs or handshakes? Are visitors welcome in your bedroom, or do you limit them to the living room? Knowing your comfort zones early on helps establish clear physical boundaries. For example, you're out dancing with

your friends, and a male friend gets too touchy. In this situation, it's essential to be assertive and communicate your boundaries clearly. You can firmly say, "Hey, I appreciate having fun with you, but I want to keep my personal space. Please don't touch me without asking first.
"

2. Social Boundaries

You have the right to your circle of friends and social activities. They're important when others push you to postpone your plans to help them or pressure you into attending parties you'd rather skip. Being firm about your preferred social activities and the people you want to spend time with is key. Recognizing which social situations you want no part of is equally important.

3. Emotional Boundaries

Your feelings are yours alone, and no one should dictate them. Whether someone says, "You should be mad" or "You should feel lucky," it's your emotions, not theirs. Establishing strong emotional boundaries means tuning to your feelings and not letting others control them.

4. Intellectual Boundaries

Your thoughts and opinions are yours to form. Don't let others tell you what to think or say about a particular situation. Trust yourself to come to your own conclusions using the information you've gathered independently. It's vital not to let another person's opinions dictate how you live your life.

KEY TAKEAWAYS

- Being assertive is a must, especially for girls
- People will try to push you around or take advantage, but don't let them
- You have to set boundaries and stand your ground without being rude
- Always be firm and confident in expressing what you want and need
- It's about being true to yourself and not letting others walk all over you
- So, don't be afraid to speak up, and be assertive when communicating your needs

Chapter 8
Overcoming Perfectionism

"If you look for perfection, you'll never be content."

- Leo Tolstoy

You have probably heard the saying, "Nobody is perfect," quite a few times. Everyone knows that perfection is unattainable, yet many never stop chasing it. Maybe the images you see online of people traveling, going to nice places, and achieving their dreams at a young age, made you believe that some people can have perfect lives. No one has an easy life. You usually see the result, but you don't know the battles they fought to get where they are today. They work hard so they can go on expensive vacations and bleed and sweat to achieve their dreams. Yet, they don't have perfect lives. People don't post their struggles online. They only post their happy moments, so you can never really know what happens behind closed doors.

Chasing perfection is like chasing a mirage. You waste your time and energy on something that isn't real. Obsession with perfection is harmful to your mental health. You will never be happy or satisfied if you want to be perfect in every aspect of your life. Your self-confidence will suffer since you will never be able to reach the image you have in your head.

This chapter covers the impact of perfectionism on your self-esteem and provides several strategies on how to overcome it and accept yourself.

WHAT IS PERFECTIONISM?

Perfectionism is setting unrealistically high standards for yourself and the desire to appear perfect in all aspects of your life. Perfectionists usually have an all-or-nothing attitude; they will feel like failures if anything is less than perfect. They differ from high achievers since they want to achieve excellence but are satisfied even if they don't get the exact result. Perfectionists are critical of themselves and others and don't accept mistakes. Mediocrity scares them because they fear people will judge them if they aren't the best in everything.

PERFECTIONISM AND SELF-CONFIDENCE

Being a high achiever wanting to accomplish your goals is a desirable quality. However, perfectionism has a negative side as it sets you up for failure. No matter how hard you work, you will never reach this impossible image you have of your life. Young girls seek perfection from age seven, but it impacts their confidence when they reach puberty at age twelve. Although hormones affect how you view yourself, social media has a more powerful impact. Since girls constantly use their phones, they can't help but fall into comparison traps when they see others flaunting their "perfect" bodies, hair, or social life.

According to a 2016 study conducted at York St John University, perfectionism has become a common issue among young people. Nowadays, people are more competitive than ever. Thanks to social media, you are always aware of your friends and family's accomplishments and can't help but sometimes compare yourself to them. The study also showed young people feel their hard work and accomplishments don't match their high standards.

Perfectionists are solely focused on their unrealistic expectations. Even if they have other successes or achieve other goals, they will dismiss them. You know the saying, "The journey matters more than the destination?" For a perfectionist, the only thing that matters is the destination they will never reach.

Perfectionism stems from a lack of self–esteem, and dissatisfaction with life. Perfectionists associate self-worth with their image and achievements. They want to do everything right because they fear their mistakes or failures will reflect badly on them. They can't comprehend that it is normal for people to mess up, and mistakes allow them to learn and do better. Perfectionists only feel worthy when others approve of them. So, they put so much pressure on themselves to be perfect and impress the people in their lives.

Society puts a lot of pressure on girls to be perfect. Even today, when feminism has been widely discussed in the media, women and girls still can't escape the many stereotypes separating them from men. Unlike boys, girls are expected to dress, look, and speak in a certain way. Many girls secretly don't want to be perfect and would rather dress how they want and not worry about their weight. It doesn't mean they want to be slobs or ignore self-care. They merely want to be comfortable rather than chase the ideal standards set by society.

The media and advertising agencies take advantage of girls' desire for perfection. They convince them that if they use their products, their bodies, teeth, hair, etc., will be perfect. Unfortunately, many young girls are oblivious to these tactics and easily fall for them. The media significantly impacts giving girls false hope and creating unrealistic expectations. Young girls are more susceptible to external influences and easily fall prey to these mind games.

Social media, marketing agencies, and society take advantage of young girls' insecurities. Advertisements and movies often show girls with the perfect smile or hair are more desirable and happier, reinforcing the idea of perfectionism even more. The only way girls can protect themselves is by boosting their self-esteem. Moreover, confidence is the most effective weapon against perfection.

Perfectionists struggle with decision-making since they want everything to be ideal. They will take time to weigh their options to get their desired results. While it is encouraged to think hard before making any decision, perfectionists do so because they don't trust themselves. However, being able to make fast decisions is a necessary skill benefitting you in various areas of your life. Some careers depend on this ability. Can you imagine an indecisive doctor in the ER?

Interestingly, perfectionism can become its own worst enemy and provide opposite results. Since no matter how hard you try, you never achieve your unrealistic goals, so you become discouraged and stop believing in yourself. For instance, you take an art class because you love to paint. You have told yourself you will become a great painter in a couple of months. It is unrealistic for a skill that takes a long time to master.

Naturally, you will fail to achieve your goal before the deadline and make mistakes since you are still learning. Even though your teacher has told you this is normal and a part of your progress, you refuse to listen. If your painting isn't perfect, then what's the point? Eventually, you give up because you don't believe you have it in you. Therefore, perfectionism has turned from a tool that was supposed to help you achieve your goal to an obstacle hindering your progress.

Confident people believe in themselves and their abilities. They trust their instincts and know they make the right choices. Even if they make mistakes, they don't allow them to define them and can quickly move on.

Unlike perfectionists who avoid taking risks because they worry about being judged, confident girls don't care about people's opinions because they know their self-worth and don't need anyone's approval. Confident girls are more successful and happier than perfectionists because they don't stress chasing the impossible. They set realistic goals, work hard to achieve them, and also celebrate their small successes.

THE NEGATIVE IMPACT OF PERFECTIONISM

Perfectionists have low self-esteem. However, they project a confident image to the world to gain approval. Deep down, they are consumed with stress, self-doubt, indecisiveness, and fear of failure. These feelings can negatively impact mental health and well-being.

Inner Critic

Everyone has an inner voice pushing them forward or holding them back. The perfectionist's inner voice is often negative and critical - it tells them they can try all they want, but they will never be good enough or amount to anything. You have probably had similar thoughts before. Whenever a perfectionist fails to live up to their unrealistic standards, they feel anger, shame, and guilt. They don't forgive themself when they make a mistake and overreact or be extremely hard on themself,

You should also pay attention to your inner voice or thoughts and what they tell you after every setback. For instance, you fail your driving test. If your inner voice tells you, "It's okay, I can try again. It isn't the end of the world," you have healthy and positive thoughts. However, if it tells you, "You are a failure and will never achieve anything," this is your inner critic and perfectionism talking.

Losing Respect of Your Loved Ones

Since perfectionists associate their sense of self with their accomplishments when they fail, they often feel ashamed and will lose everyone's respect. Understand that the people who love you will never judge you every time you mess up or fail. They also make mistakes and know this is part of being human. Your loved ones care about you for who you are, not for the perfect image you try to convey. When you fall, they will be by your side to help you get back on your feet.

Inability to Learn

Failures and mistakes are great teachers. However, perfectionists avoid mistakes, so they deprive themselves of the ability to learn. Even when they mess up, they are too busy feeling guilty to notice the lesson to help them do better the next time and succeed.

Mistakes show you how not to do things, so you can develop a better plan to achieve your goals. They provide a learning opportunity if you only silence your inner critic and allow yourself to understand the lesson.

Avoiding Risks

Sometimes risks are necessary; they can also be fun. Perfection-ists are scared of failure, so they avoid trying new things. Their fear of making mistakes keeps them from exploring life, learning new things, and discovering new interests. They spend their lives in their comfort zone and remain stuck.

You are still young and have the whole world ahead of you. Don't allow your perfectionism mentality to keep you in a rut. Live your life, learn new skills, discover new passions, and introduce yourself to new ideas. Nothing ever grows, changes, or develops in the comfort zone.

Procrastination

Since perfectionists don't have high self-esteem, they often ques-tion themselves and their abilities. Their all-or-nothing attitude often leads them to turn down opportunities because they fear the results won't be good enough. Or, they keep procrastinating to devise ways to get perfect results and end up not finishing their tasks.

OVERCOMING PERFECTIONISM'S NEGATIVE IMPACT

Perfectionism is a personality trait you can overcome with the right strategies.

Be Aware of Your Thoughts

Perfectionism thoughts are negative because they focus on your failures rather than your accomplishments. Pay attention to your inner voice and what it tells you. Whenever you have negative thoughts, write them down to keep track of them. Read them a few times and determine where they come from. Once you realize these thoughts stem from a lack of self-esteem and negativity, you will control your inner critic and alter your thoughts.

Accept Your Mistakes

Allow yourself to make mistakes and realize that failure is only an obstacle and not the end of the road. Rather than seeing your mistakes as disappointments, accept them, learn from them, and take the opportunity to grow.

Consider learning a new skill or instrument, something you have never tried before. Rather than obsessing about being perfect, take your time to learn, make mistakes, and enjoy the experience. In time, you will see that mistakes are necessary to help you improve and grow.

Set Realistic Goals

Overcome perfectionism by setting goals you can achieve. Avoid setting unrealistic standards for yourself. For instance, if you want to lose weight and lead a healthy lifestyle, set a realistic goal weight and time frame to guarantee you will reach it. It will reduce stress and restore your faith in your abilities.

Focus on the Positives

Perfectionists focus on flaws and fail to appreciate the positive aspects of themselves. For instance, no matter how great you look, you will always find flaws in your face or body because you can't accept yourself if you aren't perfect. Instead, train your mind to always look for the beauty in you and life.

Accept Criticism

Lacking confidence makes it hard for you to accept criticism, and you take comments personally. Welcome constructive criticism because, like mistakes, it allows you to grow. Also, listen to people with more experience than you and learn from them.

Practice Self-Compassion

Practice self-compassion and avoid putting pressure on yourself. You are the only person demanding so much from you and stressing you out. Be kind to yourself and accept your limitations. It's okay if you want to be the best; just remove the word perfect from your dictionary.

EXERCISES

These exercises will teach you to let go of perfectionistic tendencies, embrace progress over perfection, and cultivate self-acceptance.

Think of a Friend

Instructions:

1. Get a pen and paper and write down the unrealistic expectations you have for yourself.

2. Now, imagine this list belongs to your best friend or younger sibling, and read it with this thought in mind.

3. Remember, this is someone you love and want to see success, so ask yourself, which of these goals are unrealistic?

4. Remove or adjust unrealistic goals. For instance, if one of your goals is to speak fluent Spanish in six months, make it a year.

5. Ask yourself, what's the worst that could happen if I apply this change?

6. Use this technique with different goals to be kinder and compassionate to yourself.

Focus on the Positives Instructions:

1. Get a pen and a journal. On one page, write all the positive comments and feedback you received from people about your actions, performance, and looks. Think of the compliments you received, even small ones like, "Your hair looks nice today."

2. On another page, write the moments you managed to succeed or accomplish a goal. Think of your impact on the people in your life, and every time you leave someone feeling better. Or the times you successfully completed a task.

3. Read the positive comments from the people in your life and think of each person. Consider spending more time with them since they can lift you up whenever you are down. For instance, if one friend always laughs at your jokes and reminds you of how funny you are, give her a call and get together. You must be around people who remind you of your positive traits to realize you are good as you are. You don't need to chase unattainable goals.

4. Now, look at the other side; this is how you view yourself. How would your life change if you believed in your positive opinion of yourself?

Practice Gratitude

Perfectionism reminds you of what you don't have. You can let go of these thoughts by reminding yourself of your blessings. Put a diary next to your bed, and before you sleep, write down the good things that happened to you today and made you smile. Write anything that comes to mind, like your best friend sending you a meme that made you laugh or eating a delicious meal. It reminds you that you don't need to be perfect to be happy because your life is great as it is.

Celebrate Your Achievements

You achieve many things every day. Sometimes, getting out of bed can be an achievement when you are struggling or depressed. Celebrate your little and big moments. Be your own cheerleader, and don't wait for someone's approval to feel accomplished. Every day when you wake up, look in the mirror and celebrate something about yourself. For instance, tell yourself, "I am proud of you for being able to smile yesterday even though you had a bad day and wanted to cry." Or, "Good job for passing a hard exam. Even though it wasn't easy, you did a good job. I am proud of you." You don't have to get an A to be proud of yourself. All your successes and achievements deserve to be celebrated.

Most people are preoccupied with their unachieved goals and never pause for a moment to pat themselves on the back for what they accomplished. Focusing on your achievements reminds you that you don't need a perfect life to be happy. You are already successful and should be proud of yourself. Celebrating your achievements motivates you to keep working hard, boosts your self-esteem, and changes your thought pattern.

This mindset shows you what matters is the journey, not the destination. You learn and grow from every success and failure. You gain experience, learn lessons influencing your growth, and become a better person.

Perfectionism impacts your mental and physical health. When you remind yourself of your accomplishments, you alter the thoughts affecting your well-being.

Perfection doesn't exist. Everything in life is crooked or flawed. There is beauty in the imperfection because it's real and unaltered. The perfectionism mentality can damage your self-esteem and stand in the way of your success. Think of perfection and confidence as two arch enemies who can't coexist, so one must destroy the other. By boosting your confidence, you empower yourself against perfectionism thoughts.

Practice the strategies and exercises in this chapter to overcome the obsession with being perfect. Love and accept yourself for who you are, be proud of it, and celebrate it every day.

KEY TAKEAWAYS

- Perfectionism sets you up for failure by creating unattainable goals
- Young girls are more susceptible to perfectionism because of the pressure society puts on them
- Perfectionism and confidence can never coexist
- Perfectionism substantially impacts your mental health and life
- You can overcome perfectionism with the right strategies
- Exercises to let go of the perfection mindset
- The significance of celebrating your achievements

Chapter 9

Mindset and Self-Belief

"Developing a growth mindset is really a journey. It's a lifelong journey of monitoring your trigger points and trying to approach things in a more growth mindset way of taking on challenges, sticking to them, and learning from them."

- Carol Dweck

Your mindset is crucial in shaping your personality. It fosters healthy self-esteem, which is vital for achieving anything worthwhile. It's conducive to formulating a winning context or perspective, not to mention harnessing a drive empowered by positive thoughts, leading to success. A healthy mindset is fundamental for coping with adversities you'll face on your path to success. A stronger self-belief enables you to face obstacles during the multifaceted process of goal setting and achieving. Persistence, and unwavering self-belief, empowers you to overcome challenges and confidently pursue your goals, helping you develop resilience. This chapter provides insight into the power of mindset and self-belief in shaping confidence and success.

CULTIVATING A GROWTH MINDSET

The most critical tenet of fostering self-belief is cultivating a growth mindset. A growth mindset means you want to learn from your mistakes. It is embracing challenges, knowing you'll persevere even after a failure, accepting constructive criticism, and learning, changing, and adapting your thoughts and actions whenever necessary. A person with this mindset is constantly engaged in fostering growth.

Below are some great ideas on how to develop a growth mindset:

Look at Your Existing Mindset

You gain insight into your existing mindset by considering how you approach challenges. For example, ask yourself whether you're a social person or work well with others. Or inquire about your leadership abilities. It helps you if you have a growth mindset. Bringing awareness to your current mindset is the first step toward growing it.

Consider Your Improvements

Think about something you can do better than before. Was there something you previously found challenging, and now you do it without a hitch? How do you think you achieved this monumental change? As the hallmarks of the growth mindset, these and similar thoughts encourage you to contemplate the time and effort you've spent to improve in specific areas.

If you can't think of an area for improvement in your life, look at something a friend or relative did to improve. Did they have a smooth path, or had to go against the odds? Consider how they reached their goals and what this says about their ability to develop their mindset.

Ask for Feedback

Whether you've been successful in your recent endeavor or not, asking people how they think you did is a superb way to develop a growth mindset. A person with a different viewpoint might offer insight into your development and areas requiring improvement. This information enables you to set realistic goals for improvement.

Rely on the Concept of "Yet"

The concept of 'yet' refers to the skills you're yet to master. You must realize there will always be skills you have not developed or honed yet. However, with work and perseverance, you'll realize these are opportunities for developing strengths and overcoming weaknesses.

Try Something New

Engaging in new activities can represent the challenge of developing yourself. You might learn to improve something you're not already good at, even if this wasn't your primary goal. Whether learning a new language, picking up a course in an unfamiliar subject, or mastering artistic skills, doing something new will make you step out of your comfort zone. Being open to acquiring new skills is a surefire way to foster growth mindsets.

Feel Free to Make Mistakes

Accept that you might make a mistake or two at the beginning of your journey. Allow yourself to fail, and then learn from your mistakes. Rather than viewing them as proofs of your ineptitude, see them as a necessary part of growth. Your missteps enable you to identify your weaknesses and lack of knowledge, so don't be afraid to make them.

Look up Examples

When striving to develop a growth mindset, it helps to look at those who already have one. Whether examples from experts or looking for success examples among your circle of friends and family, there are opportunities to learn from others. Examine what they do and how they approach challenges, and consider how you can apply similar tactics.

REFRAMING STRATEGIES TO HELP OVERCOME SELF-LIMITING BELIEFS

Below are a few handy techniques for overcoming self-limiting beliefs:

Acknowledging Negative Ideas and Beliefs

After determining which scenarios impact your self-belief the most, consider them. It entails what you say to yourself (self-talk) and how you perceive things. Positive, negative, or neutral ideas and beliefs are part of day-to-day life. Some might be conducive to specific situations, while others are not. Thoughts based on incorrect beliefs impact your self-belief negatively. Reflect on whether your (negative) beliefs are correct. For instance, you might ask yourself if you would tell a friend what you think of yourself. If not, you shouldn't tell them to yourself.

Separate Yourself from Your Thoughts

Seeing your thoughts as different entities can help dispel them. Repeat your negative thoughts over and over to separate yourself from them. Notice habitual beliefs and ideas and view them from a distant standpoint - like they were someone else's ideas. This works for in-grained beliefs you might find hard to change. Instead of attempting to change them, separate yourself from them.

Confront Negative Beliefs

Once you've identified your negative beliefs, it's time to confront them. Ask yourself if your point of view is based on real facts and makes sense in the given context. There might be another reason behind your experience, situation, or issue than what you believe. Be mindful that it might be challenging to see faults in your reasoning, especially if your ideas are based on beliefs you've taken for facts for a long time. In this case, you might see them as facts when they're not entirely true.

Here are some self-limiting beliefs you must confront:

- **Seeing things through a filter:** You see everything through a negative filter, preventing you from seeing the positives and potentially distorting your perception of people or scenarios. For instance, you might think, "I made a mess during that class presentation. Now everyone thinks I am stupid."

- **Making every issue bigger than it is:** You see everything as good or bad. For example, you tell yourself, "If I don't score high on this test, my entire future will be ruined."

- **Jumping to conclusions:** You reach a negative judgment with little or no information about the situation. For example, "My friend promised to call me back, but she didn't. I must have said or done something to upset her."

- **Changing positive ideas into negatives:** You might dismiss your achievements as insignificant or view positive experiences negatively. For example, you might think, "Of course, I did well on the interview. They made it easy, which had nothing to do with my skills."

- **Accepting feelings as facts:** Sometimes, the line between emotions and facts is very murky. You could mistake your or other people's emotions for facts. For instance, you might think, "I feel I will fail to prove what I can do. This proves I am a failure."

- **Putting yourself down:** You might always put yourself down by enhancing the flaws and mistakes you made and berating yourself for your lack of achievements. For instance, you might say, "I'm bad at this job. Of course, I don't deserve a promotion."

REFRAMING NEGATIVE SELF-TALK

Negative self-talk can be incredibly damaging, especially when it becomes a habit. As a girl or woman with different roles in society, you might be tempted to fall into the trap of believing you must always be perfect. However, perfection is impossible, and striving for it only leads to disappointment and frustration. So, reframe those thoughts into positive ones instead of letting negative self-talk bring you down. The next time you criticize yourself, step back and ask yourself if that thought is really true. More often than not, negative thoughts are based on unrealistic expectations or assumptions. Instead of accepting them as truth, challenge negative thoughts and reframe them positively.

For example, if you think, "I'm so lazy. I can never get things done in time," rather say, "I might struggle with getting everything done, but I am doing my best, and that's what matters. I know that I will improve slowly." Remember, reframing negative self-talk takes practice; it won't happen overnight. Nevertheless, with time and patience, you can shift your mindset and learn to accept yourself and your imperfections.

Changing What You Believe

The hardest part of reframing negative beliefs is putting the changes into practice.

Here are a few tips:

Embrace the Power of Optimism

Be kind and supportive of yourself. Concentrate on the positive instead of focusing on a situation's negative aspects. Tell yourself, "Even if it's difficult, I can manage it." When negative thoughts arise, challenge them by asking yourself if they are based on fact or opinion. If they are based on opinion, take a few moments to reframe the thought into something more positive and realistic. For example, if you received a low grade on a test, instead of thinking, "I'm terrible at this." reframe it as, "I struggled with this task, but I know I can improve with practice."

Learn to Forgive Yourself

Everybody gets things wrong. But mistakes don't tell the whole story of who you are. These are memories. Tell yourself, "I let my friend down once, but it doesn't mean I'm a terrible person."

Don't use phrases like "should" and "must." You'll inadvertently put too much pressure on yourself. Also, it will help you develop a more realistic assessment of what you can expect from yourself.

Focus on the Positives with Gratitude

Think about the good things in your life. Recall the strategies you've used to overcome obstacles. Take time each day to write down three things you are grateful for. It could be anything from the food you ate, the people you interacted with, or a good grade on a test. Expressing appreciation for what you have in life helps shift focus from fear or worry and builds greater self-worth. When you practice gratitude regularly, you train your brain to look for the good in situations, even during challenging times.

Evaluate Your Insights

What improvements could you make the next time for a better outcome if you had a bad experience? This will motivate you to work on yourself. Since it brings you closer to success, you should be proud of every step of your progress. For example, "Even if my idea for this new project seemed silly, my friend was interested and supportive. It indicates I'm on the right path to achieve my dreams."

Set Realistic Expectations

When setting a goal, you want everything to go as planned. However, as the due date approaches, you realize more and more things are going wrong, making you overwhelmed and stressed. Setting realistic expectations helps you avoid this issue. Instead of striving for perfection, focus on what's most important - creating a plan you can adhere to. Setting realistic expectations alleviates the pressure you're putting on yourself, and you can enjoy your success.

Here's how you can apply this technique in everyday life:

- Make a to-do list by ranking the tasks in order of importance
- Be realistic about how much you can accomplish in a day or week
- Learn to delegate tasks to others
- Let go of tasks not conducive to your goal

Create a Positive Environment for Yourself

Surround yourself with people and things bringing you joy and positivity. Seek positive relationships and communities supporting your goals and values - for instance, spending time with friends who make you feel good about yourself or participating in extracurricular activities aligning with your interests and passions.

Another invaluable tool in accepting imperfection is surrounding yourself with supportive people in a positive environment. When you feel down, having a friend or loved one reminding you of your strengths and accomplishments can make a substantial difference. It's important to seek those who don't judge you for your imperfections but rather embrace and love you for them. When you're feeling overwhelmed and doubting your abilities, having a supportive friend reminding you of when you've successfully navigated tough situations will encourage confidence in yourself. Surrounding yourself with positive influences can help you stay focused on your journey toward self-acceptance.

Practice Mindfulness

Mindfulness reduces stress and increases self-awareness. Take time each day to sit in a quiet space and focus on your breathing. Notice the thoughts that randomly come into your mind without controlling or changing them. Don't try to change them; just let them flow. Observe what's happening at the moment and acknowledge your feelings without judgment.

Practicing mindfulness exercises like meditation, breathing techniques, or yoga will soothe your mind and improve your ability to focus on the present moment, increasing positivity and well-being. You can try simple mindfulness practices like paying attention to your breath or using guided meditations to help you relax and focus.

Focus on Solutions

Instead of getting stuck on problems, focus on solutions. When faced with a challenge, consider what you can do to overcome it and take action. It will empower you and lead to positive results.

If you have trouble focusing on solutions, perhaps some self-care strategies could boost your cognition to foster better concentration. Taking care of yourself physically and emotionally is fundamental for promoting positive thinking. Engage in activities bringing you joy and relaxation, and prioritize your mental and physical health. For instance, go for a walk in nature, practice yoga, read a book, or listen to music.

Journaling

Journaling can be an incredibly powerful tool for cultivating mindfulness and personal growth. Regularly recording your thoughts and feelings gains insight into your inner world and develops greater self-awareness.

A key benefit of mindful journaling is it enables observing your thoughts and emotions without judgment. Rather than getting caught up in your thoughts or trying to suppress them, you can observe them and allow them to pass by. This practice can help you cultivate inner peace and calm and develop a greater understanding of yourself.

Find a quiet and comfortable space where you can write without distraction. Set aside a dedicated journal, take a few deep breaths to clear your mind, and connect with your inner self.

As you write, allow your thoughts and feelings to flow freely onto the page. Don't worry about grammar or perfect prose - the goal is to express yourself honestly and authentically. As you write, pay attention to insights or realizations that arise, and take note of them for later reflection.

Once you have finished your journaling session, read over what you wrote without judgment or self-criticism, observing what emerges. Look for patterns or recurring themes, and consider how these insights might apply to your life going forward.

Ultimately, the practice of mindful journaling can help you cultivate greater clarity of thought, deeper self-awareness, and greater inner peace and calm. With consistent practice, it can be an incredibly powerful tool for personal growth and transformation.

Write a Letter to Yourself

As an alternative to journaling, you can write a letter to yourself. Accept your emotions, acknowledge your weaknesses, and offer yourself compassion and understanding. Whether you feel guilty for letting a friend down or ashamed because you scored low on a crucial exam, a letter can be a fantastic avenue for releasing all that's weighing on you.

Here is how to pen a letter to yourself:

1. Address yourself kindly, like you would a dear friend.

2. Then, write about the emotions you're experiencing. For example, you can write, "I know you're feeling guilty right now."

3. Next, think about why you feel this way and let your thoughts and beliefs flow freely onto the paper. For example, "You feel you're not doing enough for your teammates, and you're worried they'll be disappointed in you."

4. Once you've embraced your feelings and thoughts, write yourself a few compassion-filled lines. Do this as if you would be comforting a friend, "It's okay to make mistakes. I know

you're doing the best you can with what you have. Be kind to yourself. Remember, you're doing a fantastic job."

5. Finally, read over your letter and reflect on the emotions you've expressed. You might feel relief or release after writing down your feelings or gaining new insight into your emotions and beliefs.

Use Positive Affirmations

Affirmations are positive statements to help change your mindset and cultivate self-acceptance. By creating affirmations, acknowledging and embracing difficult emotions, you learn to be more compassionate and kind to yourself during challenging times.

Here are examples of positive affirmations for girls and women:

"It's okay to feel worried sometimes. I know the stressful times will pass. I am strong enough to handle them."

"I know feeling anxious is a normal part of life. I allow myself to experience this emotion without prejudice or judgment."

KEY TAKEAWAYS

- Cultivating a growth mindset fosters self-confidence. Start by looking at your existing mindset and improvements

- Seek feedback from others and look at examples of how people achieved success

- Embrace new experiences and make mistakes. They exist so you can learn from them

- Merely because you're not good at something yet, it doesn't mean you'll never be

- You must first acknowledge these ideas to overcome self-limiting beliefs. If you think you can't change them, separate them from your person

- However, aim to change negative beliefs by confronting them and reframing your thoughts into positive ones

- Creating a positive environment for yourself makes dealing with the emotional rollercoaster you experience while changing beliefs easier

- Likewise, mindfulness exercises, journaling, and practicing gratitude are great avenues for developing a positive, growth-oriented mindset

Chapter 10

Sustaining Confidence and Celebrating Success

"To establish true self-confidence, we must concentrate on our successes and forget about the failures and the negatives in our lives."

-Denis Waitley

So, you've managed to build your confidence and become a self-assured person? That's a commendable achievement. It's a journey worth celebrating. However, life isn't all smooth sailing. Everyone faces obstacles from time to time. Sometimes people can be downright mean and say things that shatter your self-confidence. But you can develop unshakable self-confidence to last a lifetime. It doesn't depend on what others think of you. Failures are common; they happen to everyone. What matters is how you deal with them and the obstacles that come your way. Instead of letting setbacks define you, use them as stepping stones to grow and learn. Embrace that obstacles are an inevitable part of life. They don't make you any less worthy or capable.

Unfortunately, as a woman, you will likely encounter people (men and women) who try to tear you down. It's frustrating and hurtful, but remember, you shouldn't base your confidence on their opinions. For instance, have you ever had someone say something incredibly mean to you, like questioning your abilities or appearance? It can really baffle you, right? But you don't have to let those comments define you. Building a solid self-confidence foundation means appreciating the real you. Embrace your strengths and acknowledge your weaknesses. It's okay not to be perfect; nobody is. But being real about yourself allows you to grow and improve without pretending to be someone you're not.

Celebrate your achievements, big and small. Be your number one fan. It doesn't mean becoming narcissistic or obsessed with yourself. Instead, you will be the first person you turn to for support and encouragement. Knowing your worth and not doubting your abilities because someone said something negative is a coping mechanism you must adopt. Being confident doesn't mean you won't face doubts or fears; it means you have the resilience to face them head-on and keep moving forward. Stay humble, appreciate yourself, and manifest that unwavering confidence to weather any storm.

This last chapter teaches you about manifesting confidence to last you a lifetime. The "fake it till you make it" concept does not work when trying to create a permanent attitude.

THE NATURE OF SELF-CONFIDENCE

Self-confidence is the foundation of your inner strength, rooted in the belief in your abilities, worth, and potential. It acts as an empowering force propelling you to face challenges head-on, embrace risks, and relentlessly pursue your dreams. Think of it like a muscle; it needs regular exercise and conscious effort to grow and flourish. When you tap into the power of self-confidence, it becomes a driving force for growth and achievement. It's like a guiding star leading you to success in every aspect of your life. However, if you neglect or underestimate the importance of self-confidence, it will slowly fade away, leaving you feeling unsure and held back.

THE PARADOX UNVEILED

Self-confidence is a bit of a paradox; it's this powerful thing you must actively nurture. You have to step out of your comfort zone and embrace new experiences to keep it going. It's like a muscle; if you don't use it, it weakens and, over time, becomes useless. On the other hand, if you work on it consistently and focus on personal growth, you can uncover your true potential and tap into the incredible power of self-confidence.

1. Take Risks

Your self-confidence gets exponentially stronger when you step out of your comfort zone and take risks. If you keep well within your perceived limits, you'll never discover what your true potential can do. Every challenge you encounter will prove how capable you are and further strengthen your self-confidence. However, this does not mean you should take unnecessary risks. On the contrary, while you should get out of your comfort zone, you must take calculated risks to ensure you don't make mistakes.

2. Keep Learning

If you think you've learned all there is to learn, think again. The world has infinite knowledge, and in this modern age, you have infinite resources. Maybe you're an expert in your chosen field, but this fact will not remain constant. Every field is changing and developing at the speed of light, metaphorically. If you don't keep up with all the changing trends and new knowledge that comes to light, you'll be left far behind. Do you think your self-confidence will remain the same? No. Your confidence grows with you. You'll equip yourself with the tools to succeed as you learn new things and acquire new skills. So, embrace a growth mindset and constantly improve and adapt.

3. Have a Support System

Self-confidence might come from within, but the people and environment around you are significant in nurturing it. It's like building a web of support with folks who uplift and inspire you. When you have a solid support network of like-minded individuals, mentors, and cheerleaders, you will know you have a safety net for your confidence. When you feel down and doubtful, they'll be there to uplift and remind you of your capabilities. So, collaborate and connect with others to create an environment of positivity and encouragement. It is similar to being in a constant cheering squad where your self-confidence can thrive and grow stronger. It's okay to seek guidance and support from others; it's essential for growth. However, this by no means makes you weak or vulnerable. On the contrary, it will help you build a rock-solid foundation for sustainable self-confidence to withstand any challenge.

4. Reflect and Introspect

Self-confidence is a journey of self-discovery and requires taking moments for introspection and reflection. Essentially, when you pause to assess your accomplishments and acknowledge your strengths, you reinforce your belief in yourself. It's like yourself a pat on the back and saying, "Hey, you're doing great." Even celebrating the tiniest victories can work wonders for your self-confidence. It boosts motivation, pushing you to aim for even greater achievements - everyone loves a good celebration.

Self-reflection is not only about patting yourself on the back but also about growth. When you take the time to look at areas you can improve and take proactive steps toward personal development, you keep your self-confidence vibrant and strong. You must embrace challenges, strive for continuous growth, surround yourself with supportive people, and give yourself a high-five for your successes. Remember, self-confidence isn't fixed; it's an ever-evolving force. It thrives when you put it to use and fades away if you let it gather dust.

5. Get Rid of Your Inner Critic

You know that pesky little voice inside your head that says things like, "You're not good enough for that job. Why bother even trying?" or "There must be something wrong with me since I keep getting passed over for promotions." Yep, that's your inner critic at work. But don't worry. There's a way to tackle it.

Try this 4-step process to conquer your inner critic:

- First, identify what your critical inner voice is telling you. Recognize that these thoughts are separate from your true point of view.

- Write down these negative thoughts as if they're coming from an outsider. For example, change "I can't get anything right. I'll never be successful" to "You can't get anything right. You'll be successful." It helps you see them as mere thoughts, not facts.

- Respond to your inner critic with a more realistic and compassionate self-evaluation. Write these responses in the first person: "I might struggle at times, but I am smart and competent in many ways."

- Remember not to act on the inner critic's directives. Instead, take actions aligning with your point of view, who you want to be, and what you aim to achieve.

Following these steps, you'll hush your inner critic and gain more control over your thoughts and actions. You've got this.

6. Maintain Good Posture

Good posture goes beyond having a strong back; it boosts confidence in your thoughts. For instance, when sitting up straight, you might believe the ideas you jot down, like feeling more qualified for a job opportunity. On the other hand, if you're slouched over your desk, you might be less likely to trust those same feelings about your capabilities. Here's another relatable scenario: Imagine you're a student anxious about math. When you're slouching, you might believe your thinking is inhibited, so it's harder to believe in your calculation skills. But, when you consciously sit up straight, you'll notice you gain more confidence in your abilities to tackle those math exercises. So, it's not only about appearances; maintaining good posture can truly impact your self-assurance and confidence. Stand tall, sit up straight, and watch that inner confidence shine through in everything you do.

7. Develop an Equality Mentality

Women with low self-confidence often compare themselves to others, believing everyone else is better or more deserving. However, it's time to change that perspective. Instead of constantly comparing yourself to influencers or other people, view yourself as equal to everyone around you. It can be tough, especially with all those perfect Instagram photos floating around. But here's the truth: those images are a filtered version of someone's life, not the real deal. So, create a mental shift and embrace an equality mentality. You are as worthy and deserving as anyone else. Don't waste your precious energy wanting to be someone else. Marilyn Monroe once said, "Wanting to be someone else is a waste of the person you are." Embrace who you are, own your uniqueness, and watch your self-confidence soar.

CELEBRATE YOURSELF

When was the last time you truly celebrated yourself for something you accomplished? You often focus on your flaws and shortcomings, dwelling on what you haven't achieved rather than giving yourself credit for what has gone right. It's easy to get caught up in chasing the next goal, like reaching that ideal weight or securing that promotion, without taking a moment to appreciate what you've already achieved. You keep moving those goalposts, always pushing for more and forgetting to bask in the glory of your successes.

But, if you don't pause and celebrate each triumph, you might end up unsatisfied, always thinking you're not where you should be. It's like you're on a never-ending journey without acknowledging the milestones you've passed. So, it's time to make a change. Acknowledge your wins, big and small. Celebrate yourself for the effort you put in, the progress you've made, and the obstacles you've overcome. Embrace each success as a testament to your strength and resilience.

For example, you recently aced a presentation at work or managed to stick to your fitness routine despite a busy schedule. Give yourself a pat on the back and acknowledge your awesome accomplishments. Remember, celebrating yourself isn't about being arrogant or boastful; it's recognizing your worth and valuing your progress on your unique journey.

WHY IS IT SO DIFFICULT TO CELEBRATE YOUR ACHIEVEMENTS?

As women, you've probably heard the saying, "No one likes a show-off," so you often hold back from bragging or blowing your own trumpet. Celebrating your achievements can sometimes be seen as a negative trait. Another reason celebrating yourself is difficult is you developed a habit of being overly self-critical, always looking for what you think you're not doing well. This mindset puts you in a constant state of lack and scarcity, making appreciating your successes difficult. However, despite these challenges, there are five compelling reasons you should make a conscious effort to celebrate yourself often:

1. It Improves Your Confidence

Confidence is created by your thoughts, so if you constantly think about yourself negatively and focus on what you're not achieving, it will take a toll on your confidence. If you struggle with confidence, ask yourself: How often are you celebrating yourself? The chances are not very much, if at all. Celebrating yourself is a powerful way to counter negative thoughts and boost self-assurance. So, acknowledge your accomplishments, no matter how big or small.

2. You Inspire Others

When you feel proud of yourself and openly share that pride, it's a way of honoring your achievements and inspiring others. By showing what you've accomplished, they will see what's possible. Moreover, there's something incredibly magnetic about being in a celebratory state. When basking in that positive energy, you emit an attractive aura drawing people in. It's like your energetic frequency shifts to a whole new level than when you were hard on yourself.

3. It Helps You to Overcome Doubt

Celebrating yourself can be a powerful tool to overcome doubt, especially when you venture into something new. When you set a goal for yourself and doubt creeps in from the start, take a moment to sit down and reflect. Write out your past achievements, big and small, to remind you of what you've already accomplished and truly capable of. Acknowledging your previous successes shifts your focus from doubt to confidence. It's like giving yourself a pep talk and saying, "Hey, look at all the amazing things you've already done. You've got this." So, the next time doubt holds you back from trying something new, remember to celebrate yourself and all the incredible things you've achieved.

4. It Helps You to Focus on the Journey

People give up on their dreams too soon because they become overly fixated on the result. They keep feeling the lack of not being there yet; it can make the entire journey feel miserable. But making yourself miserable won't get you closer to your dreams. Instead, shift your focus to the journey and celebrate your progress along the way. Celebrating yourself and your achievements, big and small, brings joy and positivity to your path. It adds fuel to your motivation, reminding you that you're making strides toward your dreams. So, let go of the constant need to reach the finish line right away.

5. You Attract More in Your Life

When you celebrate yourself and your achievements, you attract more positivity and abundance into your life. Your energy flows toward what you want to experience more of. There's a saying in the world of personal development, 'Your energy flows where your attention goes.' So, if you're constantly denying yourself the feeling of pride and celebration, your energy is channeled in that direction.

Wherever your energy is focused shapes your life, so by celebrating yourself, you interrupt the negative momentum and redirect your energy toward your true desires. When you make time to celebrate yourself, you send a clear message to the universe that you're ready for more positivity and success. It's a magnet attracting more things to celebrate and be proud of.

Here are a few ways to celebrate yourself more:

1. Write Down Your Achievements

Jot down your achievements, big and small. For example, did you complete a challenging project at work or learn a new skill? Don't let your inner critic tell you otherwise. If you've come this far in life, you've definitely had accomplishments. Challenge yourself to come up with at least 25 initially.

2. Think about How You Celebrate Others

Reflect on how you love celebrating others. Perhaps you take them to dinner at their favorite restaurant, buy them a thoughtful gift, or shower them with heartfelt compliments. Now, flip that around and ask yourself how you'd enjoy being celebrated. For instance, imagine receiving praise and encouragement for your hard work or having a special treat just for you.

3. Celebrate Your Qualities

Remember, celebrating yourself isn't only about accomplishments; it's about celebrating the qualities you love about yourself. It could be how loving and compassionate you are or how persistent and determined you can be. For instance, if you showed kindness to a friend in need or persevered through a tough situation, that's also worth celebrating.

4. Make Celebrating Yourself a Conscious Practice

Make a conscious effort to celebrate yourself often. Recognize every achievement, big or small, and allow yourself to revel in your success. For example, if you completed a challenging task at work, take a moment to acknowledge your hard work and dedication. Celebrate by treating yourself to something you enjoy, like a relaxing evening with your favorite book or a delicious dessert.

5. Write Down 5 Things You're Proud of Doing Every Night

Try writing down five things you're proud of doing every night. Reflect on how well you've done that day, even if it's something as simple as spending quality time with your family or completing household chores. This practice will get you into the habit of celebrating yourself regularly and boosting your self-confidence.

So, start celebrating your achievements, qualities, and small life victories. Embrace the practice of celebrating and giving yourself the recognition and love you truly deserve. You are worth celebrating. Each achievement, no matter how big or small, is a testament to your resilience, determination, and hard work. Celebrate the courage it took to step out of your comfort zone and pursue your dreams. Whether it's a promotion at work, completing a project, or mastering a new skill, acknowledge the effort you put in and the growth you've experienced.

KEY TAKEAWAYS

- Self-confidence is a journey worth celebrating, but life has its challenges and obstacles

- Unshakable self-confidence doesn't depend on others' opinions; it comes from within

- Embrace setbacks as opportunities for growth and learning

- Don't let others' negative comments define you; appreciate the real you and embrace your strengths and weaknesses

- Celebrate your achievements, big and small, without being narcissistic

- Self-confidence is like a muscle; you must exercise and nurture it regularly

- Take risks and step out of your comfort zone to strengthen your self-confidence

- Continuously learn and adapt to keep growing and improving

- Surround yourself with a supportive network to boost your self-confidence

- Reflect and introspect to reinforce your belief in yourself and set new goals

- Silence your inner critic by challenging negative thoughts and responding with self-compassion

- Develop an equality mentality; stop comparing yourself to others and embrace your uniqueness

- Celebrate your achievements to improve confidence, inspire others, and overcome doubt

- Celebrating yourself includes acknowledging achievements, embracing your qualities, and making celebrating a conscious practice

Conclusion

Confidence is a forever journey, an unwavering path leading you to your true potential. It's a journey of self-discovery, self-acceptance, and self-love, which intertwine to create an unshakable foundation for a fulfilling life. As women, this journey can be empowering and challenging, as societal norms and self-doubt often stand in your way. However, once you learn to love yourself the way you are, there's no stopping you from soaring to new heights and unleashing your full potential.

Throughout this book, you've learned to manifest confidence, accept yourself, show yourself kindness, and be a better version of yourself. In the words of the indomitable Maya Angelou, "Success is liking yourself, liking what you do, and liking how you do it." This simple yet profound statement encapsulates the essence of true confidence. You are an unstoppable force of change when you find solace in who you are and embrace your unique qualities. Self-confidence gives you the courage to ask, demand, and create the life you want.

As you navigate the challenges life throws your way, Eleanor Roosevelt's words ring true: "No one can make you feel inferior without your consent." Your confidence is an armor shielding you from the arrows of negativity and doubt. It empowers you to stand tall even in the face of adversity. Through self-affirmation and a deep-rooted belief in your abilities, you can transcend limits and embrace boundless potential.

In this journey to love yourself, you learn the lesson of lifting one another up. Encouraging and supporting fellow women on their quests for confidence reinforces the notion that you are not alone in this endeavor. Together, you create an unyielding sisterhood inspiring you to embrace the beauty of your uniqueness and the strength in your unity. As this journey comes to a close, take a moment to celebrate the extraordinary transformation you've been through.

So, as you step out into the world, hold your head high because you are now equipped with the tools of confidence. Embrace your uniqueness, celebrate your achievements, and fear nothing. With confidence as your steadfast companion, there are no limits to what you can achieve. Confidence is your forever journey, and it begins with the love you have for yourself. There's no stopping you now.

References

(N.d.). Choosingtherapy.com. https://www.choosingtherapy.com/self-doubt/

(N.d.). Parade.com. https://parade.com/1229840/judykoutsky/confident-woman

(N.d.-a). Parade.com. https://parade.com/1229840/judykoutsky/confident-woman/

(N.d.-b). Org.uk. https://www.mind.org.uk/information-support/types-of-mental-health-problems/self-esteem/tips-to-improve-your-self-esteem/

3 powerful exercises for the introverted perfectionist. (2016, July 23). The Muse. https://www.themuse.com/advice/3-powerful-exercises-for-the-introverted-perfectionist

4 ways to boost your self-compassion. (2021, February 12). Harvard Health. https://www.health.harvard.edu/mental-health/4-ways-to-boost-your-self-compassion

57 questions to ask about body image. (2022, November 30). Enlightio. https://enlightio.com/questions-to-ask-about-body-image

6 reasons why you should celebrate success. (2015, August 1). Brilliant Living HQ. https://www.brilliantlivinghq.com/6-reasons-why-you-should-celebrate-success/

Are perfectionists truly confident? The perfectionism paradox. (n.d.). ANTI-LONELINESS. https://www.antiloneliness.com/self-development/perfectionism-confidence

Asana. (2021, November 29). 10 limiting beliefs and how to overcome them [2021] •. Asana. https://asana.com/resources/limiting-beliefs

ATR Brain Information Communication Research Laboratry Group. (2016, December 15). Manipulating brain activity to boost confidence: New breakthrough in neuroscience: Self-confidence can be directly amplified in the brain. Science Daily. https://www.sciencedaily.com/releases/2016/12/161215085902.htm

Canada, R. (2023, June 20). How to overcome self-limiting beliefs and reach your full potential. Randstad.Ca; Randstad Canada. https://www.randstad.ca/job-seeker/career-resources/career-development/how-to-overcome-limiting-beliefs/

Castrillon, C. (2020, January 26). 5 strategies to build unshakable self-confidence. Forbes. https://www.forbes.com/sites/carolinecastrillon/2020/01/26/5-strategies-to-build-unshakable-self-confidence/?sh=4e99dfee8c6f

Chatterjee, A. (2022, March 8). A compassionate guide to setting healthy boundaries as A woman. ThinkRight.Me. https://www.thinkrightme.com/a-compassionate-guide-to-setting-healthy-boundaries-as-a-woman/

Children, & Screens. (n.d.). 9 tips to help teen girls cope with social comparison on social media. ParentMap. https://www.parentmap.com/article/9-tips-help-teen-girls-cope-social-comparison-social-media

Chong, J. (2022, February 1). Low self-esteem: How perfectionism sets you back —. The Skill Collective. https://theskillcollective.com/blog/low-self-esteem-perfectionism

Confidence. (n.d.). Psychology Today. https://www.psychologytoday.com/us/basics/confidence

Cunanan, P. (2018, September 27). Female assertiveness: 5 tips for girls and women to be more assertive. Eco Warrior Princess. https://ecowarriorprincess.net/2018/09/female-assertiveness-5-tips-for-girls-women-to-be-more-assertive/

Curran, T., & Hill, A. P. (2019). Perfectionism is increasing over time: A meta-analysis of birth cohort differences from 1989 to 2016. Psychological Bulletin, 145(4), 410–429. https://doi.org/10.1037/bul0000138

Dan Matthews, C. (2020, January 9). How to identify your limiting beliefs and get over them. Lifehack. https://www.lifehack.org/858652/limiting-beliefs

Does being a perfectionist affect your confidence? – Universal Mindfulness. (n.d.). Universalmindfulness.co.uk. https://universalmindfulness.co.uk/why-perfectionism-kills-confidence/

Dominating beauty standards: 4 reasons why high beauty standards are dangerous. (2023, February 20). Times of India Blog. https://timesofindia.indiatimes.com/readersblog/awesome-reads/dominating-beauty-standards-4-reasons-why-high-beauty-standards-are-dangerous-50709/

Dweck, C. (2016, January 13). What Having a "Growth Mindset" Actually Means. Harvard Business Review. https://hbr.org/2016/01/what-having-a-growth-mindset-actually-means

Eklund, S. (2020, August 18). The comparison trap. Teen Girls Help | Girls Counseling, Therapy & Directory | Teen Strong AZ. https://iamteenstrong.com/the-comparison-trap/

Eva, A. L. (2018, May 23). Five Ways to Help Teens Build a Sense of Self-Worth. Mindful. https://www.mindful.org/five-ways-to-help-teens-build-a-sense-of-self-worth/

Fallon-Peek, N. (1566678456000). 10 questions to help you work through career self-doubt. Linkedin.com. https://www.linkedin.com/pulse/10-questions-help-you-work-through-career-self-doubt-nicole-fallon/

Fran. (2022, April 25). What is a growth mindset and how can you develop one? FutureLearn. https://www.futurelearn.com/info/blog/general/develop-growth-mindset#:~:text=A%20growth%20mindset%20is%20a,The%20New%20Psychology%20of%20Success.

Graebner, K. (n.d.). How to practice self-compassion and tame your inner critic. Betterup.com. https://www.betterup.com/blog/self-compassion

Haddad, L. (2018, February 15). Seeing Failure As An Opportunity To Learn From (And Leapfrog Into Success). Entrepreneur Middle East. https://www.entrepreneur.com/en-ae/growth-strategies/seeing-failure-as-an-opportunity-to-learn-from-and/308943

Harnessing the Power of Positive Thinking and a Growth Mindset for Career Success. (n.d.). Linkedin.Com. https://www.linkedin.com/pulse/harnessing-power-positive-thinking-growth-mindset-career/

Ho, L. (2020, July 28). 7 Ways to Boost Your Confidence and Take Action In Your Life. Mind Cafe. https://medium.com/mind-cafe/7-ways-to-boost-your-confidence-and-take-action-in-your-life-7c6ec319df18

Horton, C. (2021, September 1). 13 confidence-building exercises every woman needs to try. Clever Girl Finance. https://www.clevergirlfinance.com/confidence-building-exercises/

How can you frame and reframe your failures as learning opportunities? (n.d.). Linkedin.Com. https://www.linkedin.com/advice/1/how-can-you-frame-reframe-your-failures-learning

How perfectionism can harm your self-esteem. (n.d.). Betterhelp.com. https://www.betterhelp.com/advice/general/how-perfectionism-can-harm-your-self-esteem/

Itani, O. (2020, April 23). The Confidence Cycle: Taking Action is How You Boost Your Confidence —. OMAR ITANI. https://www.omaritani.com/blog/boost-your-confidence

Jorgensen, R. (2016, May 20). The successful woman's guide to setting boundaries – without being a bitch. Women Igniting Change; Women Igniting Change®. https://womenignitingchange.com/blog/the-successful-womans-guide-to-setting-boundaries-without-being-a/

Journaling for Positivity. (n.d.). Halo. https://halo.app/articles/journaling-101/journaling-for-positivity

Keithley, Z. (2021, July 12). 40 positive affirmations for insecurity and self-doubt. Zanna Keithley. https://zannakeithley.com/40-positive-affirmations-for-insecurity-and-self-doubt/

Kreamer, P. (2020, June 16). Perfectionism kills confidence and productivity. Productivity Uncorked. https://productivityuncorked.com/perfectionism-kills-your-confidence-and-productivity/

Lagadhir, M. (1686069002000). The paradox of self-confidence: Cultivating and sustaining inner power. Linkedin.com. https://www.linkedin.com/pulse/paradox-self-confidence-cultivating-sustaining-inner-power-lagadhir/

Lawler, M., & Gillihan, S. (n.d.). What is self-care, and why is it so important for your health? Everydayhealth.com. https://www.everydayhealth.com/self-care/

Manson, M. (2020, November 12). How to overcome your limiting beliefs. Mark Manson. https://markmanson.net/limiting-beliefs

Markowicz, J., & Psychologist. (n.d.). GoodTherapy. Goodtherapy.org. https://www.goodtherapy.org/blog/Strong-Like-Amanda-Teaching-Girls-Power-Assertiveness

McLaughlin, C. (2021, March 8). 8 high profile women on their biggest failure, and what it taught them. Mamamia. https://www.mamamia.com.au/dealing-with-failure/

middleearthnj. (2019, October 14). How to combat perfectionism in teens. Middle Earth. https://middleearthnj.org/2019/10/14/how-to-combat-perfectionism-in-teens/

MindTools. (n.d.). Mindtools.com. https://www.mindtools.com/air49f4/using-affirmations

MindTools. (n.d.). Mindtools.com. https://www.mindtools.com/ax3c2aw/celebrating-achievement

Moore, C. (2019, June 2). How to practice self-compassion: 8 techniques and tips. Positivepsychology.com. https://positivepsychology.com/how-to-practice-self-compassion/

Morillo, E. (2022, July 22). Top 77 most inspiring quotes about beauty (EMBRACE). Gracious Quotes. https://graciousquotes.com/beauty/

Morin, A. (2019, August 5). Growth Mindset: How to Develop Growth Mindset. Understood. https://www.understood.org/en/articles/growth-mindset

No title. (n.d.). Study.com. https://study.com/academy/lesson/internalizing-behaviors-definition-examples-quiz.html

North, H. L., & HLN. (2022, April 20). How to celebrate yourself as a woman. High Life North; High Life North Magazine. https://www.highlifenorth.com/2022/04/20/how-to-celebrate-yourself-as-a-woman/

Parentingteensandtweens, W. by. (2018, August 14). How to help tweens and teens avoid the comparison trap. Parentingteensandtweens.com. https://parentingteensandtweens.com/helping-our-tweens-and-teens-tackle-the-comparison-trap/

Pedersen, T. (2016, June 17). Social media and body image: What's the link? Psych Central. https://psychcentral.com/health/how-the-media-affects-body-image

Perfection Quotes. (n.d.). Goodreads.com. https://www.goodreads.com/quotes/tag/perfection

Perfectionism. (2009, September 15). Goodtherapy.org. https://www.goodtherapy.org/learn-about-therapy/issues/perfectionism

Perry, E. (n.d.). 8 ways to overcome self-doubt once and for all. Betterup.com. https://www.betterup.com/blog/overcoming-self-doubt

Rautela, C. (n.d.). My fit brain pvt ltd. https://myfitbrain.in/blog/why-self-care-is-important-for-women

refreadmitreat. (2021, December 9). The social pressures for women. Refresh Treatment Rehab San Diego; Refresh Recovery. https://www.refreshtreatment.com/the-social-pressures-for-women/

Refresh. (2021, April 15). 10 ways to overcome perfectionism. Oregon Counseling. https://oregoncounseling.com/article/10-ways-to-overcome-perfectionism/

Rice, A. (2016, May 17). Challenging negative thoughts: Helpful tips. Psych Central. https://psychcentral.com/lib/challenging-negative-self-talk

Ronin, K. (2015, January 22). 9 myths about confidence that are holding you back. The Muse. https://www.themuse.com/advice/9-myths-about-confidence-that-are-holding-you-back

Sales, M. (2019, June 27). 10 ways to sustain your confidence and lead. The Business Woman Media. https://www.thebusinesswomanmedia.com/10-ways-sustain-confidence-lead/

Salters-Pedneault, K. (2011, January 27). Internalized symptoms with BPD include depression and social issues. Verywell Mind. https://www.verywellmind.com/internalizing-425251

Santos, J. (2022, February 19). 15 body positivity activities: Love your body unconditionally. But First, Joy; But First, Joy LLC. https://butfirstjoy.com/body-positivity-activities/

Schlossberg, M. (2016, May 16). The world's highest-paid supermodel says her success has nothing to do with looks. Business Insider. https://www.businessinsider.com/gisele-bundchen-says-her-career-wasnt-based-on-her-looks-2016-5

Schuy, M. (2022, November 21). Self-acceptance – how to accept myself 12 exercises & tips. CleverMemo - The Best Coaching Software for Sustainable Results and a Thriving Business. https://clevermemo.com/blog/en/self-acceptance-how-to-accept-myself/

Scott, E. (2006, May 8). Perfectionism: 10 signs of perfectionist traits. Verywell Mind. https://www.verywellmind.com/signs-you-may-be-a-perfectionist-3145233

Self-compassion is healthier than self-esteem - Kristin Neff. (2011, June 26). Self-Compassion. https://self-compassion.org/why-self-compassion-is-healthier-than-self-esteem/

Self-Doubt Quotes. (n.d.). Goodreads.com. https://www.goodreads.com/quotes/tag/self-doubt

Self-Esteem and Young Women. (n.d.). Ojp.Gov. https://ojjdp.ojp.gov/sites/g/files/xyckuh176/files/pubs/gender/treat-2.html

Shahida Arabi, M. A. (2016, May 17). How to build confidence as a woman I. Psych Central. https://psychcentral.com/lib/the-self-confidence-formula-for-women

Shahida Arabi, M. A. (2016, May 17). How to build confidence as a woman I. Psych Central. https://psychcentral.com/lib/the-self-confidence-formula-for-women

Shields, A. (2019, February 28). 10 ways to practice body positivity. Well-Being Trust. https://wellbeingtrust.org/bewell/10-ways-to-practice-body-positivity/

Susan. (2023, January 16). 85 daily affirmations to change your negative thoughts. Sassy Sister Stuff. https://www.sassysisterstuff.com/affirmations-for-negative-thoughts/

Tarteelakram. (2023, February 8). Embracing Failures as Opportunities for Growth and Learning. Medium. https://medium.com/@tarteelakram354/embracing-failures-as-opportunities-for-growth-and-learning-974519d73f26

Tewari, A. (2022, July 14). 100 powerful body positive affirmations for loving your body. Gratitude - The Life Blog. https://blog.gratefulness.me/body-positive-affirmations/

Thompson, S. (2017, May 16). Need a Confidence Boost? Research Shows Taking Action and Failing Often Will Help. Inc. https://www.inc.com/sonia-thompson/science-says-taking-action-and-failing-often-will-increase-your-confidence.html

Tips for Cultivating a Positive Mindset. (2021, June 16). Harmony. https://www.grwhealth.com/post/tips-for-cultivating-a-positive-mindset/

Topping, A. (2016, October 3). Girls as young as 7 feel pressure to be pretty – body confidence study. The Guardian. https://www.theguardian.com/lifeandstyle/2016/oct/04/girls-as-young-as-7-feel-pressure-to-be-pretty-body-confidence-girlguiding-study-reveals

Toussi, S. (2020, April 24). 10 Massive Actions to Build Confidence —. Sami Toussi. https://www.samitoussi.com/blog/10-massive-actions-to-build-confidence

Training the brain to boost self-confidence. (2016, December 19). Medical News Today. https://www.medicalnewstoday.com/articles/314777

Warrell, D. M. (2015, February 26). Use It Or Lose It: The Science Behind Self-Confidence. Forbes. https://www.forbes.com/sites/margiewarrell/2015/02/26/build-self-confidence-5strategies/?sh=685cac276ade

Webster, B. (2019, October 22). Female assertiveness: Stop resolving the tension. Bethany Webster. https://www.bethanywebster.com/blog/female-assertiveness/

What are internalizing behaviors? (n.d.). Betterhelp.com. https://www.better-help.com/advice/behavior/what-are-internalizing-behaviors/

Why Learning From Failure is Your Key to Success. (n.d.). Betterup.Com. https://www.betterup.com/blog/learning-from-failure

Why Mindset is Important. (2020, December 6). Transformative Visions. https://transformativevisions.com/why-mindset-is-important/

Wigmore, I. (2019, February 20). Snapchat dysmorphia. Whatis.com; TechTarget. https://www.techtarget.com/whatis/definition/Snapchat-dysmorphia

Wilson, V. (2021, October 14). Cultural expectations: How social norms influence our choices. Exceptional Futures. https://www.exceptionalfutures.com/cultural-expectations/

woman!, S. (2022, November 29). 5 ways to help your teen avoid the comparison trap. Simply Woman | Online Magazine by Crystal Andrus Morissette. https://www.simplywoman.com/5-ways-to-help-your-teen-avoid-the-comparison-trap/

Wood, K. (2021, February 1). Identifying and overcoming your limiting beliefs. Kamini Wood. https://www.kaminiwood.com/identifying-and-overcoming-your-limiting-beliefs/

Wooll, M. (n.d.). What are limiting beliefs. Betterup.com. https://www.betterup.com/blog/what-are-limiting-beliefs

Made in United States
North Haven, CT
26 February 2024